STO

ACPL ITE

DISCARDED

649.1 P211
Paris, Thomas.
"I'll never do to my kids
 what my parents did to me!"

D1046607

DO NOT REMOVE
CARDS FROM POCKET

4 - 14 - 92

ALLEN COUNTY PUBLIC LIBRARY

FORT WAYNE, INDIANA 46802

You may return this book to any agency, branch,
or bookmobile of the Allen County Public Library.

DEMCO

"I'll Never Do to My Kids What My Parents Did to Me!"

Allen County Public Library
Ft. Wayne, Indiana

"I'll Never Do to My Kids What My Parents Did to Me!"

A Guide to Conscious Parenting

Thomas Paris, Ph.D.
Eileen Paris, Ph.D.

Lowell House
Los Angeles

Contemporary Books
Chicago

Allen County Public Library
Ft. Wayne, Indiana

Library of Congress Cataloging-in-Publication Data:
Paris, Thomas.
  I'll never do to my kids what my parents did to me: a guide to conscious
  parenting/Thomas Paris and Eileen Paris.
     p.   cm.
  Includes bibliographical references and index.
  ISBN 0-929923-58-8
  1. Parent and child. 2. Parenting. I. Paris, Eileen.
II. Title.
HQ755.85.P375 1992
649'.1–dc20   91–34442
                                                   CIP

Copyright © 1992 by Thomas Paris Ph.D., and Eileen Paris, Ph.D.

All rights reserved. No part of this work may be reproduced or transmitted in
any form by any means, electronic or mechanical, including photocopying and
recording, or by any information storage or retrieval system, except as may
be expressly permitted by the 1976 Copyright Act or in writing by the
publisher.
Requests for such permissions should be addressed to:

Lowell House
2029 Century Park East, Suite 3290
Los Angeles, CA 90067

Publisher: Jack Artenstein
Vice-President/Editor-in-Chief: Janice Gallagher
Director of Marketing: Elizabeth Duell Wood
Design: Brenda Leach
Manufactured in the United States of America
10 9 8 7 6 5 4 3 2 1

Standing between our parents' generation
and our children's generation,
we lovingly dedicate this book
to both of them.

Acknowledgments

First we would like to thank and acknowledge our family of friends who have been patient, understanding, and supportive while this work was in progress: Carrie and Bruce Anders, Susan Beckman, Harvey Bogarat, Connie Call, Nansea Cross, Sara Eddy, Ellie Farbstein, John Laird Parsons, and Louise Steiner.

Thanks to Cathy Colman who advised us on one of our earliest drafts. Also, Charles Kraus, who added his insights and humor and helped us develop our voice, and Carolee Bogue for spreading the word. We would also like to acknowledge Julia Bishop McMichael for suggesting the Parenting Process as the name for our communication method. A special thanks to Ben Levine, our Ph.D. advisor, whose gentle insistence encouraged us to stay true to our social conscience. A special acknowledgment goes to Rick Sinatra, whose patience and computer skills saved us untold hours of work. He was always there when our computer illiteracy threatened to fragment us.

Thanks to Sallie Gouverneur, our agent, who saw the value of our work. She continues to advise us, reassure us, and keep us pointed in the right direction.

We want to take this opportunity to acknowledge Janice Gallagher for her initial recognition and belief in our concepts. Thanks also to Jack Artenstein and RGA Publishing.

We are gratefully indebted to Susan Golant, our editor. Her tireless work on our behalf allowed us to present our ideas in a cohesive and coherent manuscript.

Thanks to Molly Edmundson and the Midtown School, who provided a loving and supportive environment in which the seed of this book was planted.

We especially thank the parents, clients, and children with whom we have worked, for trusting us with their lives and their stories. They have been our teachers.

Tom gives special thanks to Jack Rosenberg, who has been his teacher, supervisor, and mentor. He has given Tom a model for tenacious self-discovery. Thanks to Lucinda Gray for supporting him in discovering his own legacies. To Margie Rand, who has his heart and shares his life, and who is always there for him, Tom offers a special appreciation.

Eileen gives special thanks as well to Marjorie Rand and Jack Rosenberg, her teachers, Kati Breckenridge, and especially to Beverly Morse for her love and guidance.

To Tom's parents, Gloria and Pep, and Eileen's parents, Ella and Harry, your legacies are treasures that have inspired us. To Tom's son, Adam, and our son, Seth, whose presence in our lives has helped us grow, thank you.

Contents

The Birth of the Parenting Process

We met during our early 20s and were drawn together in part by a mutual understanding of the pain we had each endured while growing up. Although our childhood experiences were essentially different, we nevertheless shared a common thread: Our respective parents had not allowed either of us to express our authentic feelings.

The book entitled *Summerhill, A Radical Guide to Childrearing* by A.S. Neill brought Eileen to work with children. Eileen had a heartfelt and intuitive response to Neill's reverence for life and children. She learned that when adults view children's unfolding development as good and support that development, youngsters learn with excitement. When adults validate and respect children's feelings, kids begin to form separate identities. Eileen also learned that when adults are authentic with children and allow honest emotional exchanges, kids become independent and learn to cooperate and negotiate individual differences.

Indeed, Neill's principles became the intellectual foundation for Eileen's understanding of what had been wrong in her relationship with her parents. Eileen was so inspired by *Summerhill* that she decided to work with children, and in 1966 she was hired as a teacher's assistant at the Midtown School in Los Angeles, an alternative school for young children from age two to age six.

Excited about her experience at Midtown, Eileen then recruited Tom. There, we were both influenced by Molly Edmundson, a teacher who taught us the importance of allowing a child's development and growth to come from within the youngster and not be forced from without. We learned from Molly to validate children's feelings, a skill called *mirroring* (see chapter 6). It was this ability to mirror children's feelings that we observed many parents lacked. Mirroring conveys an attitude of acceptance and reflection which confirms the separate existence of every developing child. Youngsters need confirmation in order to feel secure.

After the Midtown experience, Eileen went on to teach parent-toddler classes at the Los Angeles Family School. There she helped families weather separation as their youngsters first entered school. She also conducted discussion groups for parents, addressing their concerns and problems. Eventually, she started a consulting business, teaching communication skills to families.

In 1970 we were married, and four years later our son, Seth, was born. Like all new parents, we were filled with love and optimism. We made a promise never to do to our own child what our parents had done to us. However, Seth was only a year old when we realized our marriage was no longer viable. We didn't know what was wrong or how to fix it. The marriage counseling we tried didn't offer us a way to undo unconscious family patterns that interfered with our closeness. Past emotional injuries can damage adult relationships just as they can drive a wedge between parent and child. And so we got divorced.

As you might expect, separation devastated our idealism. How could we reconcile splitting up with our commitment to be good parents? A "broken home" had nothing to do with the parenting experience we wanted to provide for our year-old son. Neither of us had planned to become a single parent. We knew we wanted our son to have the best of each of us. How could we accomplish this if our marriage had dissolved?

Eileen insisted that parenting responsibilities be shared equally after the separation. She realized that her mother had had all the burden of parenting in her own family, even without a divorce. Her father had been uninvolved, except when it came to discipline. She had seen her exhausted mother become a martyr, and she rejected the same fate for herself. Besides, she didn't want Seth to grow up without a dad. She knew that with a strong father-son bond, Seth's journey into manhood would be less perilous.

At first Tom was frightened. He resisted what appeared to be an overwhelming responsibility: sharing equally the parenting of an infant after separation. Then he realized that maintaining a close relationship with Seth was a way to honor a promise he had made to himself: to establish and maintain an intimate and involved father-son relationship. When Tom was growing up, his father was uninvolved with him, and Tom had longed for this intimacy all his life. Maintaining a close relationship with Seth after the divorce was a way in which Tom could begin the healing process for himself. He would not pass on the injury of an emotionally absent father.

It was during this painful period that we made the decision to enter into a joint custody arrangement: Seth lived with each of us half the week. Unfortunately, sometimes our hurt and angry feelings toward each other interfered with our ability to negotiate our parenting differences. It was difficult and demanding to separate our many issues and conflicts. However, our early vow "not to do to our kids what our parents had done to us" bound us together and fueled our commitment to our son. We believe this is why we were able to make joint custody work.

As we struggled to sort out our love for Seth from the breakup of our marriage and its effect on our relationship with him, we made some important discoveries— discoveries that were the basis of what would later become the Parenting Process. We saw that our family was defined by the quality of our relationship with our son and not by the fact of our separation and eventual divorce. We each made a commitment to keep our past hurt and anger separate from our parenting relationship. This allowed us to make Seth's development and well-being our primary focus.

Eventually we learned that when we were able to resolve our differences, our family became an emotionally safe haven for Seth. Our positive negotiation became a model for Seth's own problem-solving and healthy functioning, not only at home but in the world at large. This made it possible for personal and family stability to develop and for Seth to become less vulnerable to peer pressure and other outside turbulence.

Finally, in raising Seth, we found that the residue of hurts and injuries from our own childhoods resurfaced when we interacted with him. We discovered what all parents experience sooner or later: Our children are the ones who can get to us the most. It is the parent-child relationship that reactivates so intensely our longings to regain the emotional pieces that were missing from our own childhood.

After our separation and the establishment of joint custody, Tom became involved in the emergent Men's Movement. This led to a commitment to work toward changing the rigid roles and stereotypes that prevent men from becoming close to their children and spouses. He focused on spousal abuse and domestic violence. Along with several other men and women, Tom was a founding member of Los Angeles Alternatives to Violence, a counseling and referral service for abusive men. As a result of this work, Tom decided to become a professional psychotherapist. He received a master's degree in counseling psychology and began his professional training at the Rosenberg-Rand Institute in Venice, California. Tom is licensed as a Marriage, Family, Child Counselor and became part of the training staff at the Rosenberg-Rand Institute. With Dr. Marjorie Rand, Tom trains other psychotherapists throughout the United States, Canada, and Europe.

As we continued to parent together, the boundaries of our relationship changed. No longer married, we recovered the part of our relationship that had worked. Our common interest in psychological healing and parenting became the basis for a friendship and professional relationship. Tom encouraged Eileen to enter graduate school. She also began professional training at the Rosenberg-Rand Institute and received her license as a Marriage, Family, Child Counselor in 1988.

We decided to deepen our education and received our doctorates in human behavior on a joint Ph.D. project in 1990. As long as we pursue our work with parents, our education will continue. We have learned so much from the children and parents who have placed their trust in us.

A number of educators, theorists, and clinicians have contributed to our education and understanding of parent-child relations. This accumulated body of knowledge and research provided us with a solid theoretical foundation for what we experienced and learned in our day-to-day interactions as parents. We would like to share with you some important contributions made by others in the fields of psychology and human development.

Dr. John Bowlby, a leading researcher and teacher of personality development, was the first to study the consequences of bonding and attachment (or its absence) on the emotional health of children (see chapter 5). Bowlby's work sparked the scientific research of Dr. Margaret Mahler, a child psychoanalyst, who studied and observed mothers and infants. Dr. Mahler theorized that the successful resolution of a child's conflicting needs for intimacy and autonomy occur as parents nurture and facilitate him through the stages of bonding and separation (see chapters 5 and 7). Dr. Mahler believed that this process resulted in the establishment of a strong, individual identity in each child.

We trained as psychotherapists at the Rosenberg-Rand Institute of Integrative Body Psychotherapy (IBP) in Venice, California. The personal and professional work that we performed at the institute allowed our parenting experience to become grounded in psychological and developmental theory and practice. During our studies at the IBP Institute, we were introduced to three psychological concepts that we transferred from psychotherapy to parent-child relationships: the repetitious nature of family relationship patterns; *fragmentation,* or the experience of losing one's composure and feeling emotionally regressed (see chapter 3); and *boundaries,* or the expression of our separate and unique feelings and thoughts (see chapter 7).

Dr. Heinz Kohut, the creator of Self Psychology, observed that in order for children to have inner resources to draw upon, parents need to respond to their emotional expression with empathy, accuracy, and understanding (see chapter 6). When parents accomplish this task, children develop a strong sense of internal identity and security. Then, during times of emotional stress, even when parents are unable to respond optimally, children will have an inner resource to fall back on.

Dr. Alice Miller, a prominent author and psychoanalyst, has written several books in which she describes what happens to children when their parents use them to satisfy their own emotional injuries. In *The Drama of the Gifted Child* (see chapter 7), she explains that when children adapt to please their parents, they cannot develop authentically.

Dr. Nancy Chodorow, Dr. Dorothy Dinnerstein, and Dr. Carol Gilligan have helped us understand how a boy's sense of masculinity and a girl's sense of femininity are influenced by the way in which the theme of separation is worked out in the family (see chapter 7). The elimination of sex-role stereotypes is more complex than simply letting girls play baseball or giving boys permission to cry.

Family therapists believe that each member of the family influences and is influenced by every other member. Individual development cannot be fully understood without looking at each of these relationships. In her book *Peoplemaking,* Dr. Virginia Satir, a pioneer in the family therapy movement, explained, "All of the ingredients in a family that count are changeable and correctable . . . at any point in time" (see chapter 2). We learned from Dr. Satir the transformative value of teaching families communication skills.

Dr. Daniel Stern, author of *The Interpersonal World of the Infant,* has had a profound effect on the field of developmental psychology. It had been thought that once certain stages of development were over, a window of growth closed. Dr. Stern, along with other researchers, has given us a more flexible and optimistic picture of development. By studying Dr. Stern, we have been able to present our parenting guidelines as pervasive and ongoing themes in the life of each child, not rigid stages of development that start and stop at specific times. It is never "too late" for parents to intervene and help their children with developmental problems.

We've applied Dr. Stern's theories to our own lives, too. In fact Tom himself thought that it might be too late for his relationship with his first son, Adam. He fathered Adam when he was 21, was never involved with him, and lost track of his whereabouts. In working with children and growing as a parent, Tom became haunted by the knowledge that he had a son somewhere. Tom realized that he had recreated his own legacy of an emotionally absent father with Adam. In fact, he had been emotionally and *physically* absent from Adam's life. Tom decided to find his son. Eventually he contacted Adam's mother and arranged a visit. Slowly, father and 16-year-old son established a relationship. At 19, Adam came to live with his dad.

Tom used the Parenting Process in their growing relationship and found that Adam responded well. The legacy of an emotionally absent father was changed. Now Tom is an actively involved father with both of his boys. His sons have their father, and the brothers have a relationship with each other that has added joy to their lives.

The joy of family life can be enhanced by conscious parenting. We believe our parenting method brings out the deep love that parents feel for their children and turns it into an expression that supports both family relationships and individual well-being.

Part I

The Legacy

1

Welcome to the Parenting Process

The distinctive characteristic of human beings is namely, to influence our own evolution through our own awareness.

Rollo May, *The Courage to Create*

At the age of 15, our son, Seth, wanted to learn how to ride a motor scooter. We arranged for him to take a state-approved class. After the first lesson, he complained that it hadn't gone very well. Worse yet, he said he wouldn't ask any more questions in class. Astonished at his anger, we wondered what had happened.

"I asked two questions," Seth replied, "and both times the teacher humiliated me in front of the other students. I need this class to get my license, and I know that I ought to speak up if I don't understand, but I just won't do it anymore."

The second class consisted of riding in the park. When we picked up Seth on the way to our friends' house, his head hung down and his shoulders slumped. Now we really knew something was wrong. As he entered the car, Eileen asked Seth what had happened. He shrugged and

3

said, "Nothing." From his demeanor we knew that wasn't true! In fact, we wanted him to talk about his feelings so we could help him with them, but he refused. This left us feeling somewhat helpless and frustrated. Nevertheless, we decided not to pressure Seth to relieve our own frustration, and so we allowed the silence to continue. We had to consciously tolerate the tension of our own unmet need to be emotionally open in order to allow Seth to come to terms with this problem himself.

Seth is a child of parents who are therapists and "parenting experts." One of the promises we'd made to ourselves was that we would raise our child to be open with us about his feelings, since we had grown up in families in which emotions weren't discussed. That was part of *our* legacy of injuries. Forcing Seth to talk to us would have been just as detrimental to him as our ignoring his concerns altogether. We wanted to create a climate in which emotions could be freely shared. This would be an authentic change from what we had each experienced. We wouldn't do to our child what our parents had done to us!

Therefore we needed to curb our impulse to make Seth share his feelings. We had to separate the hurt we had each felt at being unable to talk to our parents from the present situation with our son.

We also knew that when Seth is upset or angry, he tends to pull back. He doesn't do this out of spite but to connect with himself and sort out his own issues. We have learned to trust that when we give him the room to work out his emotions at his own pace, he will come back and make contact with us. When he is ready, Seth is quite capable of sharing his feelings. He is a sensitive young man who is basically comfortable with himself. He just has a different style and pace than we thought he would have. We had imagined that if our son had permission to be open emotionally, he wouldn't need to withdraw at all.

True to form, by the time we reached our destination, Seth appeared to be feeling better. His shoulders no longer slumped, and he was more animated. After a while, he talked at great length about the class and his anger toward the teacher. Seth told this story:

"I was having trouble kick-starting my bike. I asked the teacher if he could watch me and tell me if I was doing anything wrong. He did and then said, 'I think you have a bad attitude. If you change your attitude, the bike will start. But I think you are going to fail this class.' "

All the adults present agreed that the instructor's approach was more destructive than helpful. As a result, Seth decided to find a new teacher. He subsequently got his license without any difficulty.

This incident was a good reminder for us. Seth was not going to talk to us on our timetable in order to prove that we, indeed, had accomplished a better job of parenting than our folks had or to compensate for our own feelings of loss.

On the other hand, when we consciously interrupt our legacy of injuries, we also learn how to interact with our children without repeating our own past. In our family we knew that one of our legacies involved the impossibility of sharing feelings with our parents. This awareness alerted us to ways in which we would expect Seth to act more openly in his relationship with us.

Ironically, it is within the parent-child relationship that our own early childhood pain is most likely to resurface. Whenever our children pressure us to meet their needs, they can reactivate our own unmet childhood longings, our legacy of injuries. Without realizing it, we try to get our sons and daughters to parent us! When our children "behave properly" by, say, sharing their feelings when we want them to, we feel protected from experiencing old hurts. You may be dealing with similar issues in your family. If your mom or dad never paid attention to you, you may feel the same hurt feeling inside today when your child doesn't listen. This legacy of children reactivating parents' old injuries is handed down in succeeding generations. Indeed, had we required our son to talk to us, ignoring his need to set his own pace, he might have withdrawn from us even further. Unconsciously we would have reinforced the scenario in which we had grown up: children being unable to talk to parents.

As parents, it is helpful to identify our childhood injuries, because they will inevitably reemerge as longings for our own children to behave in ways that would repair our old pain. If we parent from our childhood neediness, we miss our children's real experience in the moment and become incapable of recognizing and validating their emotions. When that occurs, children feel misunderstood, and parents, in turn, feel frustrated.

"I'll Never Do to My Kids What My Parents Did to Me!"

Ideally a family is a haven, a place in which children grow and become their best selves. As parents we want to create a refuge for our children, an environment of trust and well-being that provides them with an emotional safety net for the trials and hardships of growing up.

Our need to create such an environment may partially explain our desire to have children in the first place. Perhaps we longed for a loving, safe atmosphere when we were children.

What happens to our good intentions, however, when we're in the heat of battle with our kids? What about the fierce commitment we've made to ourselves to be good parents? What about our resolve that we would never pass on to our children the same emotional injuries we received as children? Do we actually know how to keep these promises?

We try to provide our kids with the emotional assurances that we didn't receive when we were young. Perhaps we felt whatever connection we had with our parents was jeopardized whenever they were unhappy with us. Or perhaps it seemed that they would abandon us emotionally if they disapproved of our behavior. Perhaps we often felt misunderstood. Did our parents validate our feelings or discount and dismiss them? Were we confident about receiving attention for our deepest fears and concerns, or did we have to hide our feelings and pretend? Did we receive permission to be ourselves—to be separate and different? Finally, were we treated as unique individuals, or were we told what to like and how to feel? As parents, many of us are concerned about perpetuating these problems with our own children.

As therapists, we have learned that even though good intentions and promises to be different are important, by themselves they may be insufficient to disrupt emotional legacies from the past. You may lack the awareness of how old injuries are transmitted or even that these injuries exist. As professionals, we have learned that the first step in lasting change is always *awareness*. In order to be able to create and sustain a healthy relationship with your children, you must understand emotional injuries and how they are transmitted.

Perhaps you were often spanked as a child. The smallest infraction would result in your being hit, and as a result you grew up feeling wrong and bad. Now, as a parent, you've promised yourself not to spank your kids. When relatively minor incidents occur, however, you fly into a verbal rage. Even though you've eliminated hitting, your exaggerated reaction may cause your children to feel that they are also bad and wrong and can never please you. In addition, they might experience you as being unjust. What's worse, despite your best efforts, you will feel misunderstood, and the family emotional environment will remain essentially unchanged from that of your childhood. But the good news is that you can interrupt and change such a disheartening dynamic with the help of this book.

The Benefits of the Parenting Process

The Parenting Process will help you identify your childhood emotional injuries and how you transmit them today in your relationships with your children. We will teach you how to stay in the present moment in order to create the haven of safety and trust of a loving family. We will help you identify your old patterns of interaction and how your children trigger them.

Your awareness is an escape from the trap of handing down a fixed set of emotional injuries. Learning what your injuries are and how they occurred, in addition to understanding the emotional needs of your children, will prevent your passing on these unconscious patterns. You can get unhooked from the past.

Freeing yourself from your legacy of injuries will allow you to validate your children's feelings and set limits to keep them safe without a power struggle or a battle of wills. Once conscious of your own hidden needs, you will no longer inadvertently abandon your children emotionally. They will feel understood even in times of disagreement. And you will learn how to relate to your child's uniqueness, thus encouraging authentic cooperation rather than coercion or duplicity. Learning new parenting skills will keep the door to communication open. As your youngsters grow, they will be able to talk to you about their real and deepest feelings.

In this book, you will learn to identify your own childhood injuries and notice when they interfere with parenting. Then you can break the chain of hurt feelings handed down from one generation to the next. The sooner you identify your childhood injuries and begin to use the Parenting Process, the easier it will be for your children to grow into a well-adjusted adulthood. The Parenting Process supports your children's good feeling about themselves from the inside. This "good feeling," called a healthy sense of self, must be present in order for children to fully actualize their own gifts. With a strong sense of self, your youngsters will have a place inside themselves where they can find strength, support, comfort, and acceptance—a connection with all of life.

Conscious parenting is an important part of maturation and growth. Being a conscious parent means learning about children's emotional development, examining our own lives and our relationships with our parents, learning to admit our mistakes, and seeing the importance of a style and quality of parenting that moves between flexibility and reasonable limits.

What This Book Can Offer You

"I'll Never Do to My Kids What My Parents Did to Me!" is for all parents who want to have warmer and deeper relationships with their children—no matter how good or how difficult those relationships may be now. All children are born with emotional needs for both oneness and separateness. Some families promote individuality and self-reliance at the expense of togetherness. Some nourish family unity at the expense of individuality, leaving little room for a child's unique thoughts and feelings. In this book, we will teach you how to be both separate and connected, how to create relationship patterns that are satisfying and fulfilling. Such relationships will help you respond to a wide range of emotions and situations with your family.

In chapter 2, we explore family legacies. We discuss the origin of the compulsion to repeat family relationship patterns—all parents have this compulsion to some extent. We explain family systems theory and the many ways in which legacies can be transmitted. You will learn how individuals get stuck in family roles, are assigned emotional attributes, and are limited by injunctions regarding feelings and behavior. You will also learn the importance of modeling.

In chapter 3, we present an extensive questionnaire that you can use in two ways. First, we ask you to identify emotional "tender spots" left over from your own childhood. When reacting to your hurt feelings from the past, you become an ineffective parent. We teach you how to recover your emotional equilibrium. During the second run-through, you can use the questionnaire to become aware of how you may improve your relationships with your children.

One aspect of being a conscious parent is having the best understanding possible of children's emotional development. Indeed, parenting can be confusing without this understanding. In chapter 4, we provide an overview of the development of a healthy sense of self and the emotional ingredients that are required to nurture our relationships with our children. We explain how an internal good feeling supports each youngster's individuality and uniqueness. We also introduce the three guidelines of the Parenting Process.

In chapter 5, we explain the process of bonding, the first of the three guidelines. Creating and supporting a bond with your child is a process that extends beyond infancy. In fact, it is an essential and ongoing element of healthy parenting throughout the years. Without an emotional connection to you, your kids may have to fend for themselves before they are ready. The emotional bond we have with our youngsters is the soil in which their emotional growth is rooted.

Mirroring is the skill most often missing in parent-child relationships. In chapter 6, we explain how mirroring is the parenting skill through which children learn to identify their own emotional experience. As you learn to mirror accurately, your children will feel seen and understood.

The first experience of life for both parent and child is one of separation. This occurs the moment the umbilical cord is cut. When we have difficulty in being emotionally separate, our children suffer, as does our relationship with them. In chapter 7, we explain the paradox that only emotionally separate parents can truly feel close to their youngsters. It is also in the separation/individuation process that gender differences can become rigid and confusing. We explain how the important theme of separation is different for boys and girls. We also focus on limit setting and discipline.

In chapter 8, we combine the three guidelines—bonding, mirroring, and separation—to form a unified communication method. You will learn to use the Parenting Process to analyze your interactions with your children and get back on track when things go wrong. The examples in this chapter address common issues and conflicts that arise in family life. By learning how to negotiate differences, you will obtain the communication skills necessary to create family closeness and warmth.

In chapter 9, we look toward the future, imagining how children who have experienced flexibility and equality in their family will help create a world that reflects their positive feelings—a world in which differences between people will be resolved by negotiations. We speculate on the influence that positive, stable parent-child relationships can have on families and society.

The Growth of the Parenting Process

For more than 10 years we have been teaching the Parenting Process in workshops and seminars to parents from diverse backgrounds and family structures: single parents, stepparents, shared-custody parents, and the traditional two-parent family with children of all ages. Although each family structure seems to have its own set of unique conflicts, over time we have learned that regardless of family arrangement or socioeconomic, racial, or ethnic background, *children's developmental needs remain the same.*

Our weekend workshops are educational and experiential. Usually, 15 to 25 parents meet to talk in general terms about family legacies and how they are transmitted, the participants' individual developmental injuries, and children's overall emotional developmental needs.

Once parents have a basic understanding of emotional development, they are ready to practice the guidelines of the Parenting Process. Parents act out problems they are having with their child. During this role-playing, we teach the skills of mirroring and empathy, and parents practice separating their feelings from those of their children. Over the years, we have found that the Parenting Process transforms families, and we hope that it will transform yours, too.

2

The Family Legacy: How Emotional Patterns Are Acquired

Many of the time-honored techniques that have been passed down from generation to generation are, quite simply, bad advice masquerading as wisdom.

Dr. Susan Forward, *Toxic Parents*

*O*ur family legacy is a tapestry of conscious and unconscious attitudes that we acquire from our parents. Since some of what our folks teach us is positive while some is inadequate or downright detrimental, we may experience this tapestry of parenting perceptions and misperceptions as a family treasure, a family curse, or a little bit of both.

Your child grows up in a unique environment that is a blend of Mom's and Dad's family histories. Your child is influenced by the combination of the emotional experience, beliefs, and values that each of you brings to the task of child rearing.

For example, Fred, a father in one of our parenting workshops, acquired from his controlling mother a need to control his own children's feelings. He also learned his father's kindness and inability to express emotions. Fred was different from his mother and his father, but in the final analysis he was controlling in a gentle, passive way. He came to our workshop because his six-year-old son, Robbie, was having trouble at school. The other boys always picked on him. Robbie was unable to tell the bullies to stop. He had difficulty standing up for himself. After a parent-teacher conference, Fred realized that he needed assistance in order to help his son. The teacher recommended our workshop.

Fred had transmitted his legacy very subtly. As we talked with him, however, we began to understand his parenting difficulties and how he had learned them. Fred's kindness was genuine, but his anxiety about being a nice guy came from his childhood role of having had to care for his mother emotionally. In fact, Fred's mother had controlled his emotional life. She had told him what to do and how to feel. It was important to her that no one in the family become upset or angry, and Fred always worried about her feelings. Fred's father, on the other hand, was a mild-mannered man—kind but emotionally distant. Fred feared that the man would fall apart on the rare occasions that his dad became upset. So as Fred grew up, neither of his parents helped him to manage his own anger. Instead, he held these feelings in and never learned that anger was just another normal emotion among many.

A sensitive and warm parent, Fred worked hard at attending to Robbie's feelings, yet he communicated his fear of anger by his inability to let Robbie become upset for even a moment without his trying to make everything "all better." Robbie, in turn, was learning to take care of his dad by holding in and avoiding his anger, just as Fred had done when he was a child.

Fred came into the workshop saying, "I thought I would never do to my kid what was done to me, but here I am. What happened? How can it be that I've tried so hard to be different with my son, and I end up hurting him in a similar way?"

We explained that during interactions with our children we find ourselves in situations that stimulate hurt feelings from the past. We helped Fred see that when Robbie was upset, Fred felt more like a child than a father. When we say to ourselves, "I'll never do to my kids what my parents did to me," the promise is really a wish to avoid re-experiencing our own childhood injuries and to refrain from passing them on.

The Role of the Unconscious: Repeating Relationship Patterns

In the unconscious, time stands still. Whatever was, still is. As a parent, this means that your past feelings remain alive, ready to be triggered by events in your present relationship with your kids. You re-experience your own childhood emotions and unconsciously repeat the choices and behaviors you made when first responding to those old feelings many years earlier. This is how the legacy of parent-child relationship patterns is handed down to each successive generation.

For example, Melissa's mother had been cold and withdrawn making her feel like a bad child. Now, when Melissa's own children, Tina and Danny, sulk, she again feels like a bad child and therefore withdraws from them. So Tina's and Danny's experience with Melissa is like Melissa's experience with her own mother. Psychologists call this phenomenon *repetition compulsion.*

To one degree or another, we all are driven to duplicate our early relationship patterns. These patterns are so much a part of us that we have difficulty changing them. They become all we know or think is possible. When we first glimpse that they are recurring patterns, we still may have trouble changing. Even if they are painful, these old patterns are so familiar and ingrained that they feel safe to us, and we don't want to let them go.

Many self-help books describe this compulsion as unhealthy and even pathological. We strongly disagree with this pessimistic view. The compulsion itself is not pathological, since the re-creation of early childhood feelings is an inevitable part of human life. We should not condemn ourselves when this occurs. Instead, it's wise to be compassionate toward ourselves and understand that we are doing the best that we can. In repeating our childhood patterns, we are trying to re-create the climate in which we can meet our unsatisfied developmental needs.

Jerry, for example, had a distant, rejecting mother. Instead of looking for a warm woman to be his spouse, he will more likely seek out another cold, withdrawn woman. He will then try to get her to be warm to him in order to gain the feeling of care that was missing with his own mother. It is important for all of us to realize that beneath the repetition of relationship patterns lies the healthy desire to heal our early wounds.

In addition, it helps to understand that our responses to the emotional situations we experienced as children were our best attempts to take care of ourselves at that time. Those early attempts may not be the most effective choices today. Yet when we automatically revert to old behavior patterns, we tend to unwittingly view current situations as we did in the past. It is easy to see, then, how we might carry some old assumptions—our family legacies—into our current relationships with our kids.

When we recognize our compulsion to repeat and become aware that we are caught in old feelings, we can use our new consciousness to make more appropriate choices and responses.

Fred, for instance, was repeating the relationship pattern that existed in his family when he was a child. Fred's parents told him outright that angry and upset feelings were unacceptable. In this way Fred learned to become fearful of his angry feelings. By suppressing his anger, he acted like a "good little boy" to please his parents. In Fred's unconscious, all angry feelings were dangerous. Indeed, he couldn't distinguish the past from the present. He was afraid that when Robbie became upset, something bad would happen; Fred feared losing Robbie's love.

Fred had made a partial improvement with his own family. He never told his son that anger was wrong, but he smothered Robbie's upsetness with kindness. The behavior was new, but the message—don't feel or act angry—didn't change. Since Fred had not resolved the issue of his own anger, his attentiveness, even though it was a better effort than that of his parents, still taught his child to hold his anger inside.

When Fred became conscious of his old pattern in our workshop, he realized that he needed to let Robbie experience his upset feelings. Instead of smothering these feelings, Fred learned to listen to them. Indeed, he began to notice the fearful feelings in himself when his son was upset. But instead of acting like a good little boy by "fixing" his child's anger, he was able to be available to his feelings.

As parents, we all have unfinished emotional business that surfaces as recurring patterns. We tend to do to our children what was done to us, so if we think about the familial attitudes and behavior we didn't like as children, we can begin to see what we will be at risk of passing on, in varying degrees, to our kids. Some of the attitudes and behaviors we might convey are:

- Overprotectiveness
- Unrealistic achievement demands
- Critical and judgmental behavior
- Discounting and dismissive attitudes
- Fear of abandonment
- Fear of being engulfed
- Guilt
- Blame
- Sulking
- Shame
- Withdrawal
- Losing control
- Attitudes and beliefs about food, sex, alcohol
- Prejudices
- Controlling and emotionally demanding behavior
- Martyrdom
- Victimization

Our aim is to help interrupt some of the most destructive patterns by helping you become conscious of them.

How Emotional Legacies Are Passed On

In order to interrupt the transmission of your childhood injuries, you must identify how they were passed on to you in the first place. There are a number of ways in which families transmit legacies, including how the family functions as a system; the roles that particular family members play; injunctions that are given to kids about feelings and behavior; the assignment of attributes or personality characteristics; sex roles; and modeling. Let's look at each of these in more detail.

Family Systems

Family relationship patterns originate in our parents' beliefs about themselves and us, and in their approach to child rearing. Over time, these influences become a part of our internal reality. They color and shape the way we feel about ourselves, the way we perceive the world, and the way we experience relationships. Think of this process as a sort of family hypnosis. Much of it occurs outside our awareness. It's as if a trance is induced that colors our perceptions of ourselves and the world. For instance, if from the time we are infants our parents repeatedly tell us we are bad, we will eventually believe them. This process can be subtle or overt. But either way, over time we *internalize* our parents' views and beliefs about who we are.

Family therapists view the family as an emotional system. Rather than merely a collection of individuals, it is a self-contained unit, much like a volleyball team: players need to cooperate to further the common goal of winning the game. Only one person at a time can be designated server—otherwise there would be chaos. But differences also exist between family and team. Since families need to support the individual growth of family members, they must also be flexible. They deal with relationships and feelings. A flexible family system resembles a volleyball team in which everyone has a chance to serve. In addition, it is an open system: open to other people, ideas, growth, and learning. A rigid family system, on the other hand, is more like a team in which only one player serves. No one else has a chance. It is closed. Communication doesn't exist, or it occurs in only one direction, from parent to child. The resolution of conflicts is difficult to achieve when emotions remain unexpressed. New information, ideas, and feelings are exchanged neither among family members nor individuals or institutions outside the family unit. When children grow up in a closed family system, they internalize the rigidity and carry it with them into their own family relationships. Without awareness, they may lack the ability to be flexible and to change.

Family Roles

What is a family role? Having a role in a family is like being an actor in a play in which each cast member is assigned a specific character to portray a certain theme. In most plays, the actors cannot switch roles or characters. The characters are written before the actor is hired (or the baby is born). While an actor has some leeway (a few lines ad-libbed here and there), the framework is fixed and set ahead of time. Each night the play is presented, each actor repeats the same performance.

Instead of functioning as unique individuals, our children are sometimes assigned roles in our families, too, such as "the baby," "our little genius," or "the caretaker." Without allowance for a wide range of emotional expression, however, each role becomes a rigid vehicle that merely expresses a personality trait. Roles tend to be inflexible and inhibit children's authenticity.

Family roles become important in our relationships. Just as in a play the same performance is repeated night after night, so in a rigid family system, conflicts tend to recur regularly. Family members, unaware that they are caught in roles, often fight about the same issues for years, with the same unsatisfying outcome.

A healthy family system has the flexibility to support the optimal functioning and developing maturity of each adult and child. A dysfunctional family system, on the other hand, depends on each person's limiting who he is to the predetermined role in order to serve the family system. When a person tries to grow in a rigid system, other family members often pressure him to stay in the same role, because any change threatens the family equilibrium.

When roles are strict, they tend to be handed down and can thus perpetuate a family legacy. In fact, family roles are so compellingly influential in transmitting family legacies that it is important to notice when you are caught in one or have assigned a certain role to your children. Below are some of the more common roles. You may recognize yourself or other members of your family as the following:

"Bad boy" or "bad girl"

"Good boy" or "good girl"

"The baby"

"Our little genius"

"The caretaker"

"The mediator"

"Dummy"

"The favorite"

"You should have been . . . (a boy, a girl)"

Let's examine these in more detail.

Good Boy or Good Girl

Good boys and girls are "little angels." They never misbehave and always comply with authority. They get excellent grades and have perfect manners. Their teachers often recognize them and recommend them as examples to their peers. So what's the problem? Paradoxically, it's normal for children to act out and test their parents' limits to some degree in the course of growing up. Children who do otherwise often behave for their parents' benefit, not their own. They tend to grow into adults who have a weak sense of their authentic identity and often lack passion and creativity. Good boys and girls may be followers, not leaders, and they may be excessively controlled by others' opinions of them, because they have only learned to act for the sake of pleasing others.

Quite often good boys and girls reverse themselves during adolescence and act out as teenagers. This occurs because adolescence is a developmental period during which the child's major issue is forging an identity separate from his parents'. Because good children have complied with parental expectations all their lives, the only way they can now have a separate identity is to explore the rebellious side of their nature.

Bad Boy or Bad Girl

The label of being a bad boy or girl can be applied very early in life. Exploring the world and testing limits is a normal part of growing up for all children. However, when we see our children as bad because they exhibit some acting-out behaviors, the prophecy can become a self-fulfilling one.

Jean, Billy's mom, first assigned the role of bad boy to Billy when he was only two years old and she was pregnant. One day while at the playground, Jean became tired and wanted to return home to take a nap. She explained this to Billy, but he was uncooperative; indeed, he had a tantrum. Jean was upset that Billy didn't understand her needs, even though his behavior was normal for a two-year-old. It was then that she decided that Billy was a bad, selfish child. From that moment on, whenever Billy didn't cooperate or agree with Jean, she told him he was a bad boy. Billy grew up believing he was a bad person. As an adult, he was troubled by a constant feeling of shame.

The Baby

The baby of the family is often, but not always, the youngest child. The baby has the privilege of being the immature one of the family. These children are treated as special. Their family always takes care of them, and they never have to grow up. When a child is designated the baby, his parents forgive him more easily and more often. They expect less of him, and he rarely has to accept the full consequences of his behavior. Babies are adored and cherished and are the center of attention.

When the baby grows up and tries to establish adult relationships, he often has difficulty giving up his role. He expects others—spouses, coworkers, and his own children—to put his needs first and to make him the center of attention. In fact, babies who become parents want their children to take care of them instead of the other way around.

Nina's mother, Elaine, was the baby in her family. Now, as a parent, Elaine expects Nina always to put her first, otherwise she is terribly wounded. As the baby, Elaine was never required to delay gratification.

Children who are compelled to parent their own parents tend to take care of everyone's feelings but their own.

Our Little Genius

A "little genius" is a child whose parents elevate and exaggerate his accomplishments. Of course, it is important to be excited as your child grows and achieves a new developmental milestone. Your kids thrive when you acknowledge their growth and development. However, the role of our little genius can be so distorted that it presents children with a clouded and unrealistic picture of themselves.

When the role of our little genius is assigned, a baby's first smile might be interpreted to mean that he will grow up to be a comedian, or his first step is proof that he will be a long-distance runner. Such distortions can place tremendous pressure on children to perform miracles and to achieve higher and higher goals, even though these may be beyond their developmental reach.

In one of our workshops, a mother and father were concerned about their five-year-old son, Jimmy. While learning how to print, he had been told time and again how smart and perfect he was. Now, he was so anxious every time he made an imperfect letter that he tore up his paper in a tearful rage. As you will learn in chapter 6, children need to be reflected accurately, so they have permission to be beginners and make mistakes. Children who are given the role of genius suffer from unreasonable expectations to perform and never feel satisfied about their real accomplishments.

The Caretaker

Most of us are familiar with the role of caretaker. When one family member is assigned the task of being responsible for the emotional well-being of the others, he or she is the designated caretaker. To some degree, we all have the capacity and desire to care for others, instead of focusing our attention exclusively on our own needs and feelings. It is important for us to develop the ability to empathize. We must be able to set aside our feelings and see to the needs of others when it is appropriate. For example, if you are tired and your baby is sick, you set aside your tiredness and see to your child, because she is unable to fend for herself.

When caretakers sacrifice their emotional life for that of another, however, the consequences are detrimental to their well-being. You may have heard the word *codependency,* a term derived from the treatment of alcohol-impacted families. Codependency is an attempt to define what happens when we inappropriately adopt the role of caretaker toward a loved one struggling with a chemical dependency. Codependency is now used in a larger context. It is a term that is interchangeable with caretaker. Any family member who *automatically* sets other family members' welfare ahead of her own could be called codependent. Being a caretaker can deprive those we are trying to support of the opportunity to become responsible for their own behavior. This dynamic of being inappropriately cared for often puts children in the role of victim. These kids will blame others for their own difficulties and never learn to solve their own problems.

For example, Michelle didn't remember to go to the library to take out a book for her school report. Because her mother worked in the evenings, her older sister, Elizabeth, was Michelle's caretaker. Elizabeth went to the library for her, after she was in bed, and nearly wrote the report herself, so Michelle wouldn't receive a bad grade. This attempt to help actually deprived Michelle of a learning experience, because she didn't have to face the consequences of her behavior. When a child is continually rescued, this inappropriate caretaking tends to perpetuate the child's underlying feelings of helplessness.

Mediator

The mediator is a variation of the caretaker. The mediator's task is to be aware of everyone's feelings in order to avoid conflicts. When conflicts and differences do occur, the mediator smooths things over and makes everyone happy. In families that are fraught with conflict, it is common for children to assume this role, acting as referees for their parents. Children who are mediators grow up feeling guilty and responsible for their parents' unhappiness, especially if the marriage ends in divorce.

Dummy

There are other names for this role including "screw-up," "clumsy," "forgetful," or "stupid." Kids are labelled "dummies" when they don't meet their parents' expectations. Eventually such children learn to get their parents' attention by becoming incapable of doing anything right. It is a sad truth that for children negative attention is better than none at all. It is important for you to remember that making mistakes is a part of life. When we constantly criticize children and assign them a negative role, they begin to feel that the criticism is true.

It seemed that every time Drew turned around, either his mom or his dad was calling him stupid. Now, as an adult, he lacks confidence and doesn't expect much of himself. This debilitating role has kept Drew from taking such risks as educating himself or expanding and improving his work skills. Drew found himself going from one dead-end job to another, unable to break this cycle, because he believed the role that had been assigned to him as a child.

The Favorite

The favorite child is the one who always seems to get the most loving attention. She can do no wrong. The favorite tends to be either the firstborn or the last.

Liza was born after her parents had gone through one abortion and one miscarriage. She was the child they had waited and prayed for. Neither her younger brother nor her sister could compete for Liza's prized position in the family, no matter what their accomplishments.

Whenever there is a favorite in a family, the other siblings may feel overlooked and neglected, an emotional injury that can last well into adulthood. The role of the favorite engenders discord, envy, and jealousy in other family members.

The favored child, however, is not always the most fortunate. Because this child is the center of attention, she receives the lion's share of the family legacy. If that legacy is predominately negative, she may become an emotionally troubled adult.

You Should Have Been . . . (A Boy, A Girl)

Many children have the role of being the wrong gender. Their parents had hoped they would be the opposite sex. No matter what they do or who they are, they always feel that something about them isn't right. Sharon's dad, Philip, for example, had three sisters. He had always longed for a brother. When his wife was pregnant, he prayed that the baby would be a boy. When Sharon was born, Philip had to hide his disappointment, even from himself. Philip was a loving father, but his relationship with Sharon was characterized by rough play and sports. Sharon grew up with the uneasy feeling that any of her interests that were feminine such as playing house, dress-up, or ballet, didn't garner her father's approval. Sharon always felt she had to prove herself to her father; it was imperative that she be better than all the boys in the neighborhood. This colored her experience of herself. As an adult, she always felt that she was somehow defective.

Sex Roles

Sex roles are rigid cultural and family expectations that predetermine how boys and girls are supposed to act and feel. The beliefs that surround the stereotypes are also handed down as legacies. From birth, boys and girls are expected to act and feel in certain prescribed girl and boy ways. In general, our society expects little girls to be sweet, soft, compliant, sensitive, emotional, passive, and interested in learning how to be housewives and mommies. In the 1950s, young women went to college to get their "Mrs." degree. Little boys, on the other hand, are expected to be aggressive, rough-and-tumble, stoic, unemotional, tough, and capable. The rigidity of these expectations can be so extreme that they become stereotypes. Certain behaviors can even be expressed in society as clichés, such as "big boys don't cry" or "girls are overly sensitive and dramatic."

The hospital where Tom was born, for instance, presented new baby boys with a football, whereas new baby girls received nothing. While this unequal acknowledgment might not exist today, deeply held beliefs and prejudices do change slowly.

Because sex roles are so restrictive, they don't allow for authentic human expression at variance with the script. We believe that much of sex-role behavior is learned in the family system and is supported by the social culture in which each family exists. Determining which gender differences are innately biological and which are learned and changeable is complex and difficult. It is beyond the scope of this chapter. It is clear, however, that through awareness and conscious parenting, there is much that we as parents can do to broaden the opportunity for emotional development beyond the bounds of sex-role stereotyping.

Long-lasting and real change must begin within our families. Complying with rigid sex roles robs both boys and girls of the opportunity to achieve a sense of wholeness. Once we become aware of our beliefs and prejudices, we can support our children in experiencing the full range of their emotional expression. Only then we will raise girls and boys to be both soft and strong, gentle and capable, connected and independent.

The Assignment of Attributes

When we attribute certain exaggerated qualities to children, we can miss many of their other qualities. We may characterize them in ways that are positive—such as the smart one, the pretty or handsome one, the athlete, the funny one—or negative, such as the clumsy one, the spoiled one, the silly one, the stubborn one, the sick one, the quiet one, the loner, the angry one, or the selfish one. Parents may notice and reinforce any behavior that might express the characteristic in question. They may even ignore qualities that don't fit the preconceived picture.

Donna's parents, for instance, always told her she was beautiful—"just like her mom." Donna felt limited by her sense that her appearance was the only special thing about her. Consequently, Donna didn't feel special for who she was, just for how she looked. She became insecure. Preoccupied with her appearance, Donna found it difficult to trust that her accomplishments and her friendships were based on her other fine qualities.

When an attribute becomes the whole identity for a child, the legacy that he or she passes on will be distorted in one way or another. In Donna's case, for instance, her mother transmitted to her a preoccupation with appearance. When Donna became a parent, however, she took the opposite approach. She paid little attention to her daughter's appearance, and her daughter learned to feel unattractive. Melinda believed that she could never compare with her beautiful mother.

Injunctions

Injunctions are messages that tell kids how to think, feel, or behave. These are strong commands that may be outside our awareness. We internalize these messages. They become part of who we are as parents and how we believe our children should feel and behave. Thus, injunctions, too, are handed down to each succeeding generation. They can be specific or quite general. Sometimes we give injunctions directly, and sometimes we imply them by our nonverbal attitudes. Do you recognize any of your feelings or beliefs in the following list of common injunctions?

DON'T FEEL . . . OR DON'T BE . . .	BE OR FEEL . . . (at all times)
Sad	Happy
Angry, mad, and upset	Good
Loud, noisy	Bad
Excited, alive, rambunctious	Nice
OK or happy	Entertaining
Different	Careful
Sexual	Quiet
More successful than your parents	Cooperative
Pretty or handsome	Pretty or handsome
Smart	Smart
Creative	Creative

Modeling

Modeling is a form of social learning that occurs through observation. You teach your children family patterns by modeling them. In fact, kids learn much more by watching what you do than by listening to what you say. You may model sex roles, moral values, ways of relating, thinking styles, problem-solving techniques, and social skills. This transmission of a legacy can be positive as well as negative. For example, when you model positively, you tell your children that girls and boys are equal, and then split chores with your spouse fairly, rather than down traditional gender lines. Your behavior—not your words—is what your children learn, remember, and integrate.

Indeed, your kids are very perceptive when it comes to ferreting out discrepancies between what you say and what you do. Mitch and Connie had been married for 10 years and had two children, Samantha and George. It had been a stormy marriage: Connie and Mitch couldn't agree on anything, nor were they able to resolve their differences when they had arguments. Conflicts always seemed to end with either Connie or Mitch storming out of the room and slamming doors.

When Samantha and George had differences, however, their parents said, "You have to learn to get along with each other; why don't you two cooperate?" Samantha and George, at ages nine and seven, respectively, noticed the discrepancy, so instead of doing what their parents told them to do, they duplicated the behavior their parents modeled. Thus, Samantha and George did not have the key to unlock a painful cycle of sibling bickering. It's highly probable that George and Samantha will re-create this legacy in their future relationships with adults as well as their own children.

Parents who model a wide range of activities within the family can have a profound and positive effect on their children. Jeffrey was eight years old. His third-grade class was going to do a cooking project. When the teacher made this announcement, the boys in the class all clamored, "That's girl stuff. We don't want to do it!" But Jeffrey said, "That's not true, because last week, when I had my birthday, my dad baked my birthday cake." Jeffrey's enthusiastic response gave pause to the other boys' initial resistance.

It's important as a parent to examine your own behavior. Are you modeling the attitudes, behaviors, and values that you want to instill in your children? Look at your own contradictions to discover discrepancies between what you say and what you do. This self-examination will enable you to provide clear messages and clear modeling for your children.

Oral Histories

Oral histories are the stories and exploits about our parents and other relatives that we hear as children. Family stories can support a child's sense of identity. They give youngsters a tradition and a sense of themselves in place and time. Joey's grandfather was a sea captain. While growing up, the young boy heard many tales about grandpa's brave adventures as he outsmarted smugglers and fought through terrible storms. Listening to stories of his grandfather's prowess inspired Joey and gave him a sense of himself in a tradition of bold and courageous men.

Eileen grew up hearing about the exploits of her grandmother Gussie, a Russian immigrant. Gussie had been active in the labor movement in the garment district of New York in the early 1900s. She risked her job and faced the threat of arrest to stand up for what she believed. This made Eileen proud and gave her the confidence to assert herself when she faced unjust attitudes.

Oral histories become destructive when we tell our kids things that may limit their aspirations. For instance, when Tom wanted to study music, his dad asserted, "No one in our family is musical." This made Tom feel that he lacked some mysterious, innate, and hereditary quality that was necessary to becoming a successful musician. He thought that musicianship was only inherited, not learned.

Patterns that limit our children's development can have a paralyzing effect on them. Can you think of any family systems, roles, injunctions, attributes, modeling, or oral traditions that have limited or supported your idea of what you or your children might accomplish?

We all want to raise our kids in a way that will open possibilities to them, and we consciously try to support their budding identities. But we all have a certain set of values and belief systems that we bring to the task of child rearing. It is important not only to examine these current values and attitudes that we are likely to pass on, but also to look back into our own past. By so doing, we become aware of the history of our feelings, emotional needs, and patterns. We can thus make conscious choices about the legacy we leave our children.

3

The Family Legacy: Becoming Aware of What You Received from Your Parents

It is the rule that parents reestablish old ties with their past through their children.

T. Berry Brazelton, M.D., and
Bertrand G. Cramer, M.D.,
The Earliest Relationship

Now that you know how emotional legacies are transmitted, let's begin the rewarding work of understanding your personal legacy and how it affects your children. All of us have memories and experiences that we treasure and others that are painful and that we wish to keep buried. While we enjoy recalling birthday parties and picnics at the beach, we may resist digging up incidents in which we felt alone, abused, or angry. Indeed, parents in our workshops often ask us, "Why should I unearth my painful memories? I don't want to live in the past. I don't want to blame my parents. I just want to be a good parent now!"

It is, however, exactly those memories and experiences that lie outside of our awareness that we will most likely pass on to our children. Only by becoming aware of our personal legacies from the past can we make new and better choices and decisions today with our children. Learning not to do to your kids what was done to you is a process that includes education, awareness, and understanding. As you learn to parent differently, you will notice an increase in your whole family's self-esteem and self-acceptance. In addition, you will all feel closer to each other.

We have designed a series of questions to help you explore the emotional climate of your childhood. As you answer these, you may notice that long-buried injured feelings resurface. This questionnaire probes areas of interaction between parent and child that have the potential to be emotionally difficult. Although such probing may be hard work, it can also be rewarding, because your renewed awareness creates an opportunity to become a more conscious parent. You reclaim old injuries and "tender spots" in the areas in which you are emotionally vulnerable. It helps to become conscious of these vulnerabilities because they are exactly the buttons your children will push, consciously or unconsciously, triggering a reaction from your past.

For example, if your answer to question 1, "Did I feel loved by my parents?" is no, you are likely to overreact if your daughter, in a moment of frustration, yells, "I hate you, Mommy!" Rather than taking your child's statement as an expression of her momentary emotional state, you are likely to interpret this message through your concern about feeling unloved by your parents and now by your child.

As you learn more about yourself, you will be less likely to respond unconsciously to messages instilled by your parents and triggered by your kids. In addition, as your awareness of your specific injuries grows, it will become easier for you to respond to your child's current emotions, rather than to your own emotions originating in the past. Otherwise, you will find you try to obtain from your children the emotional support you didn't receive from your parents.

When Howard was a little boy, his father was emotionally and physically distant. Howard longed for his daddy to play with him, and to hug him. As a father, Howard tried to give his children exactly what he didn't receive—lots of warmth and hugs. That's great! But Howard was unaware he was also trying to get from his children the warmth and hugs that he never received from his father. Much to Howard's dismay, however, there were times, especially if his children were involved in play, when they weren't interested in physical affection. At such times, Howard's childhood injury resurfaced, and he once again felt lonely and rejected. If Howard could become aware of his emotional longings, he would be less likely to pressure his children to fix his past, and his children would have the flexibility to feel like giving hugs or not, without injuring their father.

Identifying Your Own Family Legacy

We recommend that you write your answers to the following questions directly in this book. When you go through the questions, pay attention to the emotional response and any memories that accompany your answer, and write these down too. Thus, you will begin to identify those emotional areas in which you are vulnerable.

Feeling Loved

The questions in this section will help you explore the quality of the attachment you had with your parents. In order to experience a strong bond with any family member, you must feel loved, wanted, cared for, and accepted. While we all need to hear the words "I love you," it is the emotional tone of loving acceptance that we all depend upon. This emotional tone is an energetic feeling. If your parent says "I love you" through clenched teeth, you will not feel loved. But if your parent brushes your hair gently and affectionately, the emotional tone communicated is one of love, even if the words remain unspoken.

1. Did I feel loved by my parents?

_____

_____

2. How did I know my parents loved me?

_____

_____

3. Did anyone ever say, "I love you?"

_____

_____

4. How did my parents show or express their love?

_____

_____

5. Did I long to be loved?

_____

_____

6. Who loved me (parents, brother, sister, grand-parents, housekeeper, aunt, uncle, teacher, neighbor, pets)?

_____

_____

7. Did my family give affection?

_____

_____

8. Did they often touch or hold me?

_____

_____

9. Did they want me?

_____

_____

10. Did anyone pay attention to me? Who?

_____

_____

11. Did I feel special?

_____

_____

12. Did my parents plan my birth?

_____

_____

13. Did I feel wanted in my family?

_____

_____

14. Did my parents take care of my physical needs
     (clothing, shelter, food, health)?

_____

_____

15. Did they care for me consistently?

_____

_____

16. Did my parents keep their promises?

_____

_____

17. Did my parents' work schedule, depression, or illness interrupt their care of me?

_____

_____

Emotional Support

It is important for children to experience their parents as an emotionally supportive presence in their lives. This presence needs to be steady and consistent. Emotional support means that one's feelings are listened to, acknowledged, validated, and accepted.

1. Were my feelings important?

_____

_____

2. Were my parents on my side?

_____

_____

3. Were my parents emotionally available when I needed them?

_____

_____

4. Did I feel that my parents noticed and understood my feelings?

   _____

   _____

5. Was I successful in communicating my needs?

   _____

   _____

6. Were my perceptions discounted or ignored?

   _____

   _____

7. Did I hide my real feelings?

   _____

   _____

8. Did my parents see my true self?

   _____

   _____

9. Could I pursue my own interests?

   _____

   _____

10. Did my parents "always" tell me what to do?

   _____

   _____

11. Did my parents support me when my feelings were different from theirs?

   _____

   _____

12. Did I have to rebel to be different?

_____

_____

13. Who took care of me when I was sick?

_____

_____

14. Did I get special attention only when I was sick?

_____

_____

15. Did my parents comfort me when I hurt myself?

_____

_____

16. Did I frequently feel as if I were crazy or wrong?

_____

_____

17. Did my family life make sense to me?

_____

_____

18. Were my parents confident of my abilities?

_____

_____

19. Did they support and encourage me as a beginner?

_____

_____

20. Did they support me emotionally when I failed or
    made mistakes?

    _____

    _____

21. Was I afraid as a child?

    _____

    _____

22. Did I always fear something bad might happen?

    _____

    _____

23. Did my parents reassure me when I was frightened?

    _____

    _____

24. Did I feel alone?

    _____

    _____

25. Did my parents show their feelings?

    _____

    _____

26. Did I have to act as an emotional caretaker to
    either of my parents when they were upset?

    _____

    _____

Expectations

It is normal to want the best for our children. As parents we all have expectations, hopes, wishes, and dreams that our children's performance and successes reflect their specialness. Because parents have these normal desires, it is sometimes easy for children to feel that their performance is more important than who they are. The questions in this section will allow you to examine whether or not you experienced this pressure as a child.

1. Did my parents pay more attention to my accomplishments than to my feelings?

_____

_____

2. Did I feel as if my parents' expectations of me were too high?

_____

_____

3. Did I have to perform to feel accepted?

_____

_____

4. Did I have to be perfect?

_____

_____

5. Was I able to please my parents?

_____

_____

6. Did I feel important in my family?

_____

_____

7. Did I feel that my importance was exaggerated?

_____

_____

8. Did my parents allow me to be successful?

_____

_____

9. Did they allow me to know more than they did?

_____

_____

10. Did they prohibit me from surpassing a successful parent or sibling?

_____

_____

11. Did they expect me to surpass a successful parent or sibling?

_____

_____

Discipline

There are three discipline styles: authoritarian, permissive, and authoritative. The authoritarian parent says, "Do it because I say so." The permissive parent says, "Do whatever you want." The authoritative disciplinarian, on the other hand, is consistent and logical and considers the child's point of view (see chapter 8). In uncovering your family legacy, it is helpful to identify your parents' discipline style. Often we either repeat their approach or react by adopting the opposite one.

1. Did my parents impose rules to protect me or punish me?

_____

_____

2. How did my parents discipline me?

_____

_____

3. Did my parents hit or spank me?

_____

_____

4. How often did they hit or spank me?

_____

_____

5. Did they use an object to hit or spank?

_____

_____

6. Did I get punished for crying?

_____

_____

7. Did my parents punish me by withholding their love?

_____

_____

8. Did they punish me by refusing to talk to me?

_____

_____

9. Did they yell or scream at me?

_____

_____

10. Did my parents punish by criticizing or calling me names?

_____

_____

Family Conflict

Conflict and disagreement are a normal part of family life. Kids can tolerate dissention when arguments are resolved. It is when family fighting continues without resolution that children become insecure and frightened. When emotional tension and disagreement is glossed over or unacknowledged, it will become a family legacy.

1. Did I hear or see my parents engage in physical fights with one another?

_____

_____

2. Was anyone physically or psychologically injured in these fights?

_____

_____

3. Did my parents talk about or explain their disagreements to me in any way?

_____

_____

4. Did I have the role of mediating their disagreements?

_____

_____

5. Was I beaten up or controlled by any other family member (including siblings)?

_____

_____

6. Did my parents lose control when they were angry?

_____

_____

7. Did my parents or a sibling call me names or tease me often?

_____

_____

Sex Roles

Sex roles can have a profound influence on children's lives (see chapter 2). Children learn much about their gender identity through their relationships with both parents.

1. What did I learn about my masculinity or femininity from my parents?

_____

_____

2. Was it comfortable to be a boy/girl in my family?

_____

_____

3. Were men in my family allowed to feel frightened or dependent?

_____

_____

4. Were women allowed to be strong, smart, and independent?

_____

_____

5. If my parents had had different values about male/female behavior, how would that have changed their relationship to me?

_____

_____

6. Was I born the "wrong" gender? If so, how did that affect my view of myself in the world and the choices I've made?

_____

_____

7. Did I admire my same-sex parent and want to emulate him/her?

_____

_____

Sexuality

Adolescent sexuality is a normal part of growing up. Historically, children have been left alone to struggle with emerging sexual feelings and physiological changes. Our own experience during adolescence and our parents' beliefs and values regarding sexuality are important aspects of a parenting legacy that we should become aware of. In addition, many children were sexually abused without recognizing this fact. Parents who have repressed their childhood abuse may have difficulty providing loving support and clear information to their youngsters as they become sexual beings. If these questions (or the questions on drugs and alcohol) trigger memories that have been unexamined, it is important to consider seeking professional attention from a qualified therapist or an appropriate support group.

1. Did my parents accept my sexual feelings as a young man or woman during puberty?

_____

_____

2. Did anyone touch or fondle me in a way that made me uncomfortable or that I now know was inappropriate?

_____

_____

3. Did I have to keep it secret?

_____

_____

4. Did I feel safe?

_____

_____

5. Did my family keep secrets about sex?

_____

_____

6. Did I learn that sex was a normal part of life?

_____

_____

7. Did my relationship with either of my parents change dramatically during adolescence?

_____

_____

8. Was I able to talk about sex with either parent?

_____

_____

Drugs and Alcohol

Drug and alcohol abuse can affect adults' ability to parent consistently. Often, the diseases of drug addiction and alcoholism are denied or hidden in family life. When drug or alcohol abuse is present, parenting becomes a burden. Children often have to assume adult roles because parents under the influence cannot parent adequately. Because alcohol and drug use are so common in today's culture, it is often difficult to recognize when use has become abuse. For further help in determining whether these diseases of addiction exist in your family, you may wish to contact Alcoholics Anonymous or Al-Anon in your area. (They are listed in your local phone book.) AA has a checklist and other literature that can assist you in identifying alcoholism or drug addiction in your family.

1. Did my parents use drugs or alcohol often? How often?

_____

_____

2. Was drug or alcohol use hidden in my family?

_____

_____

3. Did I have to physically or emotionally take care of either parent because of his or her drug or alcohol use?

_____

_____

4. Did my parents have mood swings?

_____

_____

5. Did I feel responsible for my parents' happiness?

_____

_____

Your answers to all of these questions will inform you about the emotional climate of your childhood. They may lead you to further inquiry and exploration. You should now have an increased awareness of the positive elements of your family history as well as a better understanding of your emotional injuries. In addition, we recommend that you use a parenting journal to track your emotional response to conflicts with your children.

Using a Parenting Journal to Identify Your "Tender Spots"

To become conscious of your emotional legacy, you may also wish to keep a parenting journal to record the parent-child conflicts that repeatedly aggravate you. Simply write a brief narrative describing the incident and then record your reaction. Rate your degree of upsetness on a scale of 1 to 10.

The following is an example of a parenting journal. Joanna writes about her five-year-old daughter, Helen.

Incident	1–10	Injury or theme
Helen came home from school today and her new dress was covered with mud. I was really angry. I had told her to be careful.	7	Not being listened to
I laid out Helen's clothes. She wouldn't wear what I put out. My feelings were hurt.	5	Didn't value my opinion
I told Helen to feed the dog and she forgot. I felt exasperated.	6	My requests are ignored

When Joanna looked back over her journal, she noticed that under the heading of "injury or theme," most of her entries seemed to revolve around being discounted. When Joanna answered the questionnaire, she became aware that she had grown up with the feeling of being controlled by her mother. Her feelings were dismissed or ignored. When Joanna put this information together with her journal entries, her tender spot became clear. Whenever Helen didn't conform to Joanna's requests, Joanna relived her injuries with her own mother. She felt once more that her needs were unimportant. Because Joanna wished to avoid parenting Helen in response to her childhood injury, she learned to remind herself that her child's behavior was normal and not meant to insult her. This allowed her to separate her past from the present. Future incidents rated only a 1 or a 2 on the scale.

As you accumulate incidents in your journal, you will notice emerging patterns, common themes, and specific behaviors that upset you. Perhaps you'll find that you can handle most of your child's misbehavior but are outraged whenever she is late getting home from school or from a friend's house. Think back to your own childhood. Did anyone keep you waiting when you were a kid? Maybe Mom or Dad stayed away too long and too often, and you worried or got angry with them for disappointing you. Now, when your daughter is the least bit late, that internal panic button stimulates a strong reaction from the past.

As you accumulate journal entries, the emerging relationship patterns can document themes that cause problems between you and your children. These patterns are your legacy. You will begin to identify feelings that, though they occur in the moment of interaction with your children, were actually formed many years ago. What your children do to trigger your response may be dissimilar from incidents in your own childhood, but again your emotional reaction will be an old and familiar one. The goal of your journal is to help you separate the past from the present through awareness and to lead you to recognize that as adults we can choose to respond to our emotions in ways that were unavailable to us as children.

Sometimes, however, our emotional response to interactions with our children is so extreme that it impairs our ability to parent. We actually lose contact with the present. Psychologists call this emotionally regressed state *fragmentation.*

What Is Fragmentation?

When we lose our usual sense of well-being and self-identity, we are fragmented. Fragmentation is a physical and emotional experience, not simply an intellectual one.

The symptoms of fragmentation vary, but they include both physical and emotional responses, such as:

- Feeling helpless or abandoned.

- Feeling overwhelmed or inundated.

- Experiencing heart pounding, dizziness, blurred or distorted vision, nausea, disorientation.

- Experiencing extreme rage (including physical or verbal abuse).

If you are fragmented, your capacity to parent diminishes; you are overcome by your own feelings and longings and are unable to respond with empathy to your children's present needs.

Fragmentation occurs when you confuse or interweave your reactions to your children's behavior with your unfinished business from childhood. When Ginny saw her toddler, Timothy, trip and spill his orange juice on her new carpet, she burst into tears. As a child, Ginny's brother had always ruined her special possessions. She felt let-down by her parents because they didn't protect her things from her brother's abusive behavior. Ginny reacted to her son's mishap in the same way as she had to her brother's destructiveness.

A fragmented parent is one who is unable to make a distinction between past and present. He feels "little" and is handing down the emotional legacy he was given as a child. When your children ignore you or your requests, disagree, throw temper tantrums, pout, or talk back, their behavior may trigger a powerful and incongruous emotional response. In fact, you may feel just as small and vulnerable as they do. Obviously, you are not powerless, though you may experience yourself as such at the time.

By identifying your unresolved tender spots, however, you will be better able to understand and change any unusually strong or otherwise inappropriate reaction to your child's minor transgressions. In our family, for example, Tom has a strong reaction to being ignored because as a child he felt his dad ignored him frequently. Since Tom has explored his history, he knows this is a tender spot for him. When Seth doesn't follow through with his expected chores, such as emptying the garbage or rinsing and loading his dinner dishes into the dishwasher, Tom is susceptible to becoming fragmented. Even though these are minor incidents, sometimes for Tom they restimulate his old sense of being ignored.

Tom knows that the most effective way to handle his feelings of fragmentation is to take time out to calm down before interacting with Seth. It is important that he separate his childhood emotional response from Seth's present transgression. Then he is better able to set limits and appropriate consequences with Seth. If Tom attempts to deal with Seth when he is fragmented, on the other hand, he may hand out consequences that match his heightened emotional state instead of Seth's relatively minor offense. Inappropriate punishment would make Seth rebellious and could create a climate in which he might ignore his dad's requests all the more (see chapter 8).

If you are fragmented, it is important to "put yourself back together" before you attempt to resolve the current issues with your children. Here are some steps that can help you identify and resolve your own fragmentation:

1. Pay attention to whether or not you are experiencing fragmentation symptoms during times of intense emotion.

2. If so, stop interacting with your kids and take a time-out.

3. Send the kids into another room.

4. Take a few deep breaths, sighing as you exhale.

5. Look around the room and name 10 objects and their color in rapid succession. (This will help you bring your awareness back to the present moment.)

6. Reflect on the role your childhood wounds play in your response to your children's behavior. This is a great time to use your parenting journal.

7. Resume interacting with your children only after you have had sufficient time to calm down.

Time-outs take skill and practice. When you use the questionnaire and journal, the process of growing familiar with your own issues becomes easier and less time-consuming. As you begin to separate your childhood feelings from the present, you will become a more effective parent.

It's important, however, not to confuse all strong feelings or intense emotions with being fragmented. We all become appropriately angry at our kids at one time or another. For example, if you found your teenager driving while intoxicated, you might feel appropriately and intensely upset. It is easy for children to make us upset, since they are not born knowing acceptable safety rules or social skills. Neither are they perfect. It is our job to support their maturation process and help them develop the skills they'll need. Behavior is usually the way a child attempts to communicate feelings. When we say children are bad what we usually mean is that we are upset by their behavior, not by the essence of the child.

Adult behavior is also imperfect. Most parents try to do the best that they can and sometimes wonder if their best is good enough.

Good-Enough Parent

When you use the questionnaire and journal, you may feel the pangs of parental guilt. We know our children depend on us and give us their love with complete trust, and we instinctively respond to their helplessness with the desire that they never suffer. But in reality, we sometimes lose our temper, or we are too distracted to be compassionate. In addition, the demands of modern life on parents are very great. At one time or another, we've all wished we could have done a better job. Once, for example, when Seth was eight years old, he told Eileen that he didn't feel well and wanted to stay home from school. Eileen had a lot of things to do that day and thought Seth just wanted a day to loaf. A few hours later, however, Eileen got a call from the school nurse, asking her to pick up Seth because he was running a temperature. In addition to being sick, Seth was feeling hurt. Whenever Eileen recalls this incident, she can still feel some pangs of parental guilt.

As we learn to do the necessary detective work to interrupt damaging family patterns, we must remember that everyone suffers some emotional bruises while growing up. There are no perfect parents and no perfect kids. Parents have always known the hard work and demands involved in raising children. They have taken more than their fair share of blame for the difficulties inherent in growing up. It is important to bear in mind that all parents want to make their children happy. The purpose of the questionnaire and the journal is to raise your awareness of your history in order to improve your parenting skills. However if, you start to feel inadequate after reading the questionnaire, remember that most parents do the best job they can, and their best is generally good enough.

No one can feed a hungry baby, for example, at the precise moment of hunger each and every time. A baby will experience some frustration as a part of growing up. Obviously, good enough is a relative term. Common sense tells us that when we respond to the baby's need for food consistently (but not always perfectly), this will indeed be good enough. When you feed an infant consistently, he learns that he will receive attention when hungry. When you respond to a baby sporadically, he feels insecure. He doubts that his needs will be attended to.

Human beings are marvelous creatures. As adults we can repair our parents' mistakes. Indeed, we can learn to avoid those mistakes with our children. And when we forgive our mistakes and use them as learning experiences, we can also forgive our "good enough" children for the errors they make.

Let's return again to the questionnaire, this time to see how you are doing with your kids. You may go back through the questions once more, keeping in mind your children's experience with you. This can give you a sense of what it is like for your youngsters to be in a relationship with you. You will have a better understanding of where your parenting needs attention and where your strengths lie.

In the next chapter we will explore the emotional needs of infants and children. It is important to have an overall picture of how children develop their sense of identity. Without this big picture, we are likely to do patchwork parenting.

4

Understanding Your Child's Emotional Needs

The function of the child is to live his own life—not the life that his anxious parents think he should live, nor a life according to the purpose of the educator who thinks he knows what is best. All this interference and guidance only produces a generation of robots.

A. S. Neill, *Summerhill*

*A*fter years of professional work, we are convinced that regardless of family structure, race, educational background, economic conditions, or any other variable, the parent-child relationship must be strengthened from the inside out. Many parents approach parenting with an idea of who they want their children to be and then try to control their youngsters' emotions and behavior in order to create the imagined child. After Seth was born, for example, Eileen understood that regardless of her knowledge of psychology, child development, and communication skills, she was going to pass along her legacy of emotional injuries unless she was willing to believe that what Seth told her about his feelings was true. We must be willing to abandon our ideas about how our children *should* feel and listen to how they *do* feel.

We believe that when we support our children's natural developmental processes, their lives unfold according to an inner rhythm and harmony. But in order to restructure parent-child relations, we must first have an overview of what ideal emotional development is and the components necessary to support that growth in our children.

The Goal of Emotional Development

The goal of emotional development is a healthy identity or sense of self—an essential or core experience in the body that conveys a feeling of well-being and aliveness. A healthy sense of self gives us the ability to live our own lives, to follow our own interests, and to trust our own inner voice. Parents have always known that every child starts life with a unique and individual nature. This spark of life is like the bud of a flower. If nurtured properly the sense of self will blossom in each child. Our individual identity becomes a reference point, the inner place through which we experience ourselves, our relationships, and our world. This identity is continuous and supports our ability to deal with the ups and downs of life.

How can parents recognize when their youngsters have a healthy sense of self? Children who have strong identities:

Are self-confident.

Have self-esteem.

Are able to accept and acknowledge successes as well as failures.

Are able to feel and to express their emotions directly.

A positive sense of self is the foundation for an integrated emotional life. Children who have clear identities can recognize and express their feelings and still have empathy for others. They are people who recognize their needs for both intimacy and independence and are successful in getting these needs met.

Support in Developing a Sense of Self

Children's well-being depends on having their needs met from the outside, through their attachment to their parents and others. Mature adults, on the other hand, depend on getting their needs met from the inside through their ability to stay in contact with their own sense of self. The emotional transition from childhood to adulthood, from looking outside to looking inside, is as shaky as a toddler's learning how to stand up and walk. At first the sense of self is fragile. When you are supportive of your children, their identity develops and strengthens. We believe that your most important responsibility is the support of your youngster's emotional development. To nurture your children along this developmental path you'll need love, trust, empathy, authenticity, and physical and social stability.

Love

Parental love is a complex emotion that includes strong affection, tenderness, and devotion to the well-being of our kids. We develop the capacity to love and care for another from being loved and cared for ourselves. When your child receives and integrates your love, she acquires a reliable internal source of affection and warmth that is sufficient to share with others. In families in which love and attention are abundant (or at least sufficient), children learn to love and support each other. In families where love is scarce and conditional, siblings compete excessively and feel jealous and resentful of each other's presence. When our children experience our love directly, they feel worthwhile and special. They have a sense of hope. As parents, loving our children re-affirms our positive feelings about ourselves, life, family, and humankind.

Basic Trust

A child's need for trust begins in early infancy and is dependent upon having his basic needs attended to with love and consistency. When parents are reliable, infants begin to experience their relationships and their world as trustworthy. And as they grow older, if our children do not trust our relationship with them, they will not respect our advice and limits. When children feel that parents do not have their best interests at heart, the acting out and rebelliousness of youth becomes extreme. Trust is an ongoing theme in parent-child relationships. When basic trust is good enough, we can survive the moments when our world lets us down without crumbling in despair.

Because we took care of our son Seth consistently, he learned to trust his world. We, in turn, have trusted in his development; we believed that he would grow into an emotionally healthy and strong person. Like most teenagers, Seth is acutely aware that the world is less than an ideal place. He sees hypocrisy, environmental abuse, and corruption everywhere. He is not a Pollyanna, yet, because of an internalized feeling of basic trust, he maintains an attitude of hopefulness that allows him to be an active participant in his society.

When basic trust is not established or is fragile, our children are vulnerable to feelings of despair and hopelessness. These emotions can solidify into lifetime expectations and can color children's perceptions of events. The world becomes untrustworthy. Sometimes the only apparent way of coping is to escape into alcohol or drug abuse.

Remember that if the basic trust between you and your child has been injured, it can be repaired. Like all lifelong developmental processes, the ability to heal and strengthen the trust between you and your children is an everpresent possibility.

Empathy

Empathy is the ability to identify with another person's emotional experience without losing one's emotional perspective. Think of empathy as putting yourself in your child's shoes. It is a way to listen to your children—not only to what they say but also to how they feel.

Empathy does not mean agreement. It does mean accepting that your children are telling you the truth about their feelings. You may not concur with their perspective, but you need to accept that it is real for them. When we have an empathic relationship with our children, they feel understood, an important developmental requirement for a healthy sense of self. Instinctively, children look to us for validation in order to comprehend themselves and their own emotions.

For example, Lauren and Frank, a couple we saw in our office, had a four-year-old son, Jeremy, who hated to feel excluded from any family activity. One evening when Grandma came to visit, the four played Candyland. When the game was over and it was time for Jeremy to go to bed, he saw that his mom, dad, and grandmother were going to spend the rest of the evening playing cards. Jeremy felt left out and strongly objected to being separated from the rest of the family. Lauren and Frank had already allowed Jeremy to stay up past his normal bedtime and knew that he would have a difficult day at preschool the next morning if he was too tired. They understood that they were being loving by setting good limits for Jeremy. However, they also were empathic with Jeremy's disappointment and frustration at having to go to bed before everyone else. They said, "Jeremy, we see how left out you feel. We know it is difficult to go to bed before everyone else. And it is really time for bed now."

Frank and Lauren didn't have to give up their perspective—that is, the knowledge that Jeremy needed a good night's rest. Because they could empathize with his emotions, even as they maintained their limits, Jeremy could feel understood and emotionally accepted. He didn't have to get his way to feel loved.

Children are emotionally injured when they feel unaccepted or misunderstood. These are wounds to a child's budding sense of identity. They interfere with learning how to be intimate and independent. When children are continually injured because the people in their world never fully understand their emotions and their needs, they have difficulty taking care of themselves in relationships. Children who lack an empathic relationship with their parents are often angry and resentful. They require a lot of attention.

On the other hand, when you listen empathically you will be better able to understand how your youngsters feel. As you empathize, you create a safe environment for your children to share their emotions with you. Kids who enjoy an empathic relationship with their parents feel understood and confident in themselves. They also feel safe to share their feelings.

As the famed psychologist Carl Rogers wrote in the introduction to A.S. Neill's *Summerhill,* "When children are given a responsible freedom in a climate of understanding and nonpossessive love, they choose with wisdom, learn with alacrity, and develop genuinely social attitudes."

Parental Authenticity

Parental authenticity means being honest with your child about who you are and your own humanness. It means you have the courage to admit your mistakes and to repair emotional injuries—apologizing, for example, for overreacting to a spilled glass of milk because you were tired. Part of being a good enough parent is your willingness to say you are sorry when you are wrong and to let your children see you as less than perfect.

Indeed, it is not the mistakes we make with our children that injure them; it is the denial of our mistakes. As psychologist Rollo May explains in *The Courage to Create,* "Anxiety comes from not being able to know the world you're in, not being able to orient yourself in your own existence." When we don't admit our mistakes, our children feel confused by the difference between their perception and what we say.

When we are authentic with our children, on the other hand, we model for them attitudes of truthfulness and honesty. Children learn by example. This is why modeling is so important (see chapter 2). And honesty with our children begins with honesty with ourselves.

Only a parent who is committed to developing her own sense of self can authentically give to her children. This commitment is an ongoing process. You may have just discovered that you have a legacy from the questionnaire in chapter 3, or you may have been healing and changing through awareness of your childhood issues for years. We grow and mature by gaining insights through our experience.

We can have a relationship with our children based on authenticity when we admit our imperfections: Sometimes we are wrong and sometimes we feel defensive. For example, Tom had planned to take his oldest son,

Adam, Christmas shopping. Unfortunately, father and son were busy and had difficulty arranging a time. When they finally worked out a date, Adam got into the car and asked Tom, "How long are we going to be gone?"

Tom responded angrily, "I'm trying to do this for you. Why are you giving me a hard time?"

"Dad, I'm not giving you a hard time," Adam replied. "I just asked a simple question. You seem to be in a bad mood. I think you would have been mad at me no matter what I said!"

Tom thought for a moment and then responded, "Adam, you're right. I feel pressured. There is nothing wrong with your request to know when we will be back home." Later, they were able to laugh about this exchange and in the end had a good time shopping together.

When we are authentic with our children and allow honest emotional exchanges, our kids' sense of self includes the learned ability to be honest and straightforward in return.

When we practice authenticity, children's developmental path becomes less rocky.

Social and Physical Stability

How much of your time you are able to spend with your child and the quality of that time can be indicators of how well your youngster will develop emotionally. Therefore, it is important to address those conditions that support or interfere with your physical and emotional availability. Unfortunately, not all parents can count on having access to adequate housing, health care, economic opportunities, or even food. Obviously, the lack of these necessities can result in emotional problems for children. Deprivation and poverty injure a child's self-concept and can diminish self-esteem regardless of how authentic or empathic parents may be.

We would like to see social conditions improve so that parents can be increasingly available to their children. Youngsters thrive in environments that are safe and reliable.

Our experience and expertise consists of teaching family members how to develop close, supportive relationships with each other. However, please don't interpret our belief in strengthening the family as a call to return to the intact nuclear family. Children can be as emotionally injured in a traditional home as in any other family arrangement. And conversely, emotionally healthy children with a strong sense of self may develop in any type of family structure. Children will be emotionally healthy as long as the adult caregivers attend to such developmental components as trust and empathy. We know from experience that parents can learn to relate more effectively to their children, and that they can interrupt the emotional legacies handed down to them, no matter what the family arrangement.

The Sense of Self and the Parenting Process

When you are attentive to your children's emotional development, they will grow from utter dependency to autonomy and appropriate interrelatedness with others. Children who enjoy a healthy sense of self have the ability to adapt to today's world and to the changes inherent in personal relationships.

Love, trust, empathy, parental authenticity, and physical and social stability are the ingredients of your child's healthy sense of self. When we cook, however, simply assembling all of the ingredients does not result in a perfect chocolate cake. We also need a recipe, a way to put the ingredients together. Our recipe for conscious parenting—the Parenting Process—is composed of three developmental themes and three corresponding guidelines. They are:

BONDING

GUIDELINE 1: PROTECT THE BOND; DO NOT THREATEN EITHER EMOTIONAL ABANDONMENT OR INVASION.

MIRRORING

GUIDELINE 2: MIRROR AND REFLECT YOUR CHILD'S FEELINGS WITH EMPATHY.

SEPARATION

GUIDELINE 3: REMEMBER THAT YOUR CHILD IS SEPARATE FROM YOU, WITH SEPARATE THOUGHTS AND FEELINGS.

You will need specific information about each of these developmental themes, since each entails tasks to be accomplished by both parent and child. In part 2, we will devote a chapter to each theme. The parenting guidelines that accompany these themes provide a communication method that supports growth and heals injuries. The Parenting Process is a simple and effective tool for nurturing and strengthening your children's sense of self. It will help you interrupt your emotional legacies and add joy and vitality to your relationships with your children.

Part 2

The Parenting Process

5

Bonding

Bonding, whatever you may have heard to the contrary, is not instantaneous; there is no magical moment or even a specific time period in which the link is forged.

Kathryn Karlsrud, M.D.,
Parents Magazine, July 1989

The Parenting Process
Guideline 1: Protect the bond; do not threaten either emotional abandonment or invasion.

Bonding is the process by which parent and child become connected, intimate, and attached to each other. It takes place during many different interactions. We bond when we touch, hold, and make eye contact with our children. Infants also bond through the recognition of our faces, the scent of our hair and skin, and the tone of our voice. Bonding is a dialogue between parent and child that begins even before a baby is born and continues for a lifetime. We never outgrow the need for secure attachments.

Emotional ties are created by an exchange of love, which in the beginning can not happen without physical contact. Ideally, through consistently warm emotional and physical interactions with our children, we create a climate of safety and trust. As we tend to our children in this caring way, they begin to internalize the fundamental feelings of safety and trust.

When our children experience a secure attachment, they can venture out into the world and survive occasional disappointment. Their safe and secure relationship with us has helped them develop inner resources to which they can retreat for comfort.

A couple at one of our parenting workshops told us the following story about their eight-year-old son's ability to comfort himself when someone let him down: Ben had a secure bond with his parents. He wanted to learn how to play tennis from his grandfather, who, unfortunately, was not a great teacher. Instead of instructing and supporting Ben, his grandfather was impatient and critical, harshly pointing out the boy's every wrong move. As a result Ben neither learned how to play tennis, nor had any fun. When he returned home, his parents asked him how the tennis lesson went. Ben said, "Grandpa is not a very good teacher. He tries to teach by yelling, but I know that I'm just a beginner." Ben's parents were surprised at their son's wisdom and his ability to support himself. Ben carried within himself the love and trust that his parents felt for him and could draw on those good feelings whenever he needed support.

Children will bond when care-givers are emotionally available. Mothers, fathers, brothers, sisters, and grandparents—even baby-sitters—bond with children. The essence of bonding is a responsive *attitude* of caring and empathy. Researchers have demonstrated that bonding arises from emotional contact and availability. Although emotional availability is an attitude, it cannot be consistently conveyed unless you spend real time with your child. All family members present can participate in the bonding process.

The Beginnings of Bonding

Some early theoreticians suggested that bonding is a well-defined stage of infant development beginning at birth and ending at approximately six months of age. We believe bonding starts when you daydream about having children. You imagine what your children will be like and how you are going to feel as you love and care for them. The intensity of these loving thoughts grows when you become pregnant, and both mother and father feel the stirrings of an empathic attachment to the developing fetus. In fact, both parents have an innate nurturing instinct. This biological response to the imagined and real helplessness of the growing fetus forms the basis for the care-giving that will be required of you after your baby is born.

During pregnancy, the mother's body automatically takes care of the fetus, nurturing, warming, feeding, and protecting it. After the infant is born, however, nothing is automatic. Unlike newborn mammals that are able to scamper away from danger, human babies enter the world with intelligence but no capacity to fend for themselves, other than the ability to express distress. If parents ignore their infant's physical helplessness, the child will not survive. If parents respond only to their infant's physical needs, the child will be emotionally damaged.

As parents respond to their infant's helplessness and distress by providing comfort, food, and protection, they are treating their baby's needs almost as their own. Thus the psychological bond begins to replace the lost physiological oneness that existed in utero.

Tuning in to Baby's Early Personality

Recent infant research, especially that of Daniel N. Stern, professor of psychiatry at Cornell University Medical Center and author of *The Interpersonal World of the Infant,* published in 1985, suggests that each infant has some experience of separateness from birth onward.

Psychological closeness must include your awareness that your baby is also a separate person. Children need to experience both oneness and separateness from the very first days of life, as they do when they mold to our bodies and then stiffen, or gaze at our faces and then withdraw. When we provide a consistent bond, infants are able to move between oneness and separateness more easily, allowing themselves the intensity of contact and stimulation that they can comfortably tolerate. When our interactions with our babies include a sensitivity to the signals they send, we create security for them. This dance between parent and child is called *attunement.*

Attunement is the ability to read, align with, and match your children's emotional and/or physical state. You respond to your infant's expression with an expression of your own that corresponds to his. This happens when you mimic your baby's sounds, facial expressions and behavior. Attunement means joining with the infant's experience.

In *The Interpersonal World of the Infant,* Dr. Stern explains attunement as follows:

A nine-month-old boy bangs his hand on a soft toy, at first in some anger but gradually with pleasure, exuberance, and humor. He sets up a steady rhythm. Mother falls into his rhythm and says, "Kaaaaa-bam, kaaaaa-bam," the "bam" falling on the stroke and the "kaaaa" riding with the preparatory upswing and the suspenseful holding of his arm aloft before it falls.

When we tune into our babies' early personalities, we allow their uniqueness to unfold in an environment of acceptance and love.

Bonding with Older Children

We view bonding as an ongoing, lifelong process. As such, we can incorporate guideline 1, "Protect the bond; do not threaten either emotional abandonment or invasion," into our parenting style at any time, regardless of our children's ages. Human beings live in a web of relatedness with others. None of us are emotionally self-sufficient. We never outgrow our need for attachment. Intimate and supportive relationships depend on a strong bond. Because a healthy bond is a human need, we must always be aware of the quality of the connection with our children no matter their age or stage of development.

For example, Tom's 23-year-old son, Adam, doesn't like to travel by plane and worries when Tom must do so. He always requests that Tom phone him when Tom reaches his destination. In this way, Adam is reassured about Tom's safety, and the bond between father and son remains intact. So, from infancy through adulthood, bonding is the foundation that supports the developing relationship of children to parents, other family members, and eventually, to independent interactions outside the family.

Conversely, when we misalign, misread, or mismatch our children's signals, they may become distressed because they experience the disparity as abandonment (too little contact) or invasion (too much contact). Let's examine more closely what happens during these two situations in which bonding breaks down.

Abandonment

An episode of the TV show *Nova* entitled "Life's First Feelings" showed an experiment that demonstrates emotional abandonment between a mother and her newborn. The mother looks at her baby; the baby comes alive and coos. As the mother continues to maintain eye contact, we see the baby smile. His eyes sparkle. Obviously excited, he makes happy, gurgling sounds. The mother is then instructed to stop smiling and adopt a cold, disinterested stare, with no expression whatsoever on her face. We see the infant gaze longingly back at her mother, trying to gain her attention. When he is unable to do so, the infant turns his head and looks away momentarily. Once more the baby tries to reestablish the warm and alive interaction of a few moments earlier. He looks at his mother's face and attempts to initiate contact by smiling and cooing. The mother remains unreachable and expressionless. Finally, the infant turns his head away in despair, his face becomes lifeless, and he begins to drool.

This interaction is moving. It is a clear demonstration of the importance of your infant's experience of himself in relation to you. It also demonstrates how your children depend upon your emotionally involved interactions for their reassurance, excitement, and aliveness.

The same can be said of older children. Ginger, a mother at one of our parenting workshops, related the following story:

Ginger spent an afternoon at the park with her five-year-old, Susie. Overwhelmed by the demands of being a single, working mother, Ginger had managed to squeeze in some late afternoon time with her daughter but only by bringing paperwork home from the office. Even though she had taken some time with her daughter, Ginger was already feeling the pressure of the work that lay ahead that evening. Because she was anxious, she didn't allow enough time for Susie to make an appropriate transition from playing in the park to going home when they had to leave. Instead, she said abruptly, "It's time to go now!" Naturally, Susie began to put up a fuss, but Ginger had little patience for whining. She shouted, "If you don't get in the car this minute, I'm going to leave you here in the park by yourself!"

Susie obeyed but was quiet and withdrawn all the way home. Ginger, on the other hand, felt relieved and even satisfied that her threat had worked. This mother didn't understand, however, that although she had controlled Susie's behavior for the moment, she had injured the bond between them by threatening abandonment. Susie complied with her mom out of fear, and as we all know, fear is an unhealthy basis for a relationship.

How might Ginger have handled this conflict otherwise? Rather than resorting to damaging threats, Ginger could have given Susie several warnings that their time in the park was almost up before making the demand that they go to the car immediately. This would have prepared Susie for the eventual ride home. She still might have resisted leaving on her mom's schedule, but she would have had an opportunity to make a reasonable transition. In addition, Ginger neglected to stand by her limit without threatening. When parents feel uncertain about what to do, they often revert to idle threats. Promises to call the reform school, the police, or the bogeyman are all threats of abandonment that stem from parental desperation and fragmentation.

Under the pressure of circumstance, we may all feel conflicted between our own needs and our children's emotional demands. Children who are not securely attached or whose attachment is threatened by fear of abandonment grow up to be anxious and demanding. By using guideline 1 of the Parenting Process, however, we remember that the bond is *always* primary. In order not to threaten the bond, you need to find conscious solutions to the conflicts that arise during parenting.

When we are conscious to preserve the bond with our children, they feel safe in their relationship with us. Instead of tension and conflict, we can all experience more love, fun, and play as our kids grow and mature.

Invasion

The episode of *Nova* mentioned earlier illustrated parental invasion as well as abandonment. A mother used a rattle to stimulate and excite her infant and to engage him in mutual play. After a few moments of having the rattle shaken directly in front of him, the infant reached his limit for stimulation. He broke the contact by turning away from his mother and the toy. Instructed to ignore this cue, the woman moved the rattle in front of the baby's face again. Once more, the baby turned his head away. The mother repeated this sequence several times. Finally, the baby gave up. He became listless, averted his gaze, and began to drool.

As this experiment illustrates, babies need to be in charge of regulating the intensity and quality of the interactions with their parents as much as possible. Indeed, children of all ages must be able to control the level of contact with us. They even need permission to withdraw from contact if they so choose. Otherwise, your child's all-important feelings of safety, trust, and well-being—the building blocks of a healthy sense of self—will be wounded. And the bond between you and your child will be injured.

When you tell your kids what to say, what to think, and especially how they should feel, you are invading them psychologically and injuring the bond between you. During this invasion, they lose their sense of independence or separateness.

A friend of ours, a junior-high-school counselor, passed on the following story about parental invasion told to him by one of his students:

Chris, a seventh grader, was having trouble with his homework. Needing help, he complained to his dad, "I can't write this story for English. I don't know what to write about. Can you give me some ideas?"

Chris's father, Glenn, responded, "Sure. How about using our fishing trip?"

"Great idea!" Chris exclaimed. "I'll write about that."

"But first you have to make an outline," Glenn added. "Let me show you how." He proceeded to review their whole trip on paper. Glenn also became excited. He told Chris that he liked being asked for help, and he related how well he had done in English composition as a junior-high student himself. Glenn turned to his son. "You'll need a good opening sentence. How about . . ." He supplied what was, indeed, a good leading sentence.

By now Chris had withdrawn, but Glenn was so caught up in his own feelings and needs that he failed to notice his son had disappeared emotionally and intellectually. By the time he had finished dictating what was, in effect, his version of the fishing trip, Chris had become sullen. Glenn couldn't understand Chris's lack of enthusiasm or appreciation for the help he had provided.

Many well-meaning parents inadvertently invade their children and are confused by their children's withdrawn behavior. After all, like Glenn, these parents are trying to help. If Glenn had noticed Chris's withdrawal and acknowledged it by saying something like "Chris, you've become very quiet. Do you feel that I've taken over?," Chris would have had the opportunity to inform his dad of his feelings.

Withdrawal is a common response to invasion. When parents acknowledge that an invasion has taken place and then back off, children will usually come forward on their own. When parents are conscious of the ways that they may be invasive, children feel intimacy is safe.

Double Trouble: Abandonment Coupled with Invasion

Children's fear of emotional abandonment and emotional invasion are present at the same time, just under the surface of our interactions with them. This means that it is possible for your youngsters to feel simultaneously abandoned and invaded.

Ann is an eight-year-old third grader. Her parents, Denise and David, came to one of our parenting workshops because Ann kept getting into trouble at school. She hit other kids whenever she was frustrated. Denise, a quiet, shy, and somewhat frightened 36-year-old mother, explained that she was unable to "control" Ann and was at a loss about what to do. She admitted that she didn't like conflict. Denise's parents had divorced when she was young, and she had endured their constant fighting. Now, whenever Ann became angry or frustrated, Denise relived her difficult childhood and became frightened and fragmented. In her fragmentation, she felt helpless.

David, on the other hand, felt angry about the whole problem and was quite sure that he knew exactly what Ann needed. His solution was to spank Ann when she misbehaved at school. He was certain that his daughter would learn to stop hitting if the punishment was severe enough. His attitude wasn't surprising, since David had had an authoritarian father who believed in the adage "spare the rod and spoil the child." After many years, David had idealized his father and had come to believe that the punishment he received had actually helped to curb his own impulsive behavior, with little emotional consequence to him. Sadly, children who have been hit, spanked, or abused often feel they deserve their punishment. Unconsciously they believe that if they are punished, they must be bad, even when they don't understand why, or even if the punishment seems unjust.

Corporal punishment—spanking, slapping, shaking, or pushing—is the most invasive discipline a parent can administer. (In fact, practices that were historically acceptable as a parent's prerogative, such as hitting with an object or with a closed fist, are now reportable to the police or protective services as child abuse.) Children experience being hit as an injustice. Their innate sense of right and wrong is offended. Besides, kids are acutely sensitive to the mixed messages they receive from their parents. They understand that statements such as "I'm going to hit you and hurt you so you will learn that hitting is wrong" make little sense. Even very young children know that two wrongs don't make a right.

In fact, when Seth was about two-and-a-half years old, Tom learned this very poignantly. In our office, he told David the following story: "Occasionally, when I would lose my patience or become distressed with Seth's behavior, I would spank him. Seth had always reacted to these spankings by feeling hurt and angry. One day when I spanked him, Seth, in a tearful rage, hit me back. This infuriated me, and I spanked him again for hitting me. Then he struck me again.

"Finally Seth stopped me in my tracks. Looking up at me through his tears he said, 'Daddy, it's not fair for you to hit me and I can't hit you back!'

"The clear, honest truth of his statement overwhelmed me, and I picked him up, held him in my arms, and told him I was sorry. I said to Seth, 'You know what? You're right. Let's make an agreement. No hitting allowed in this family.' I never again spanked Seth, nor did he ever have to lash out and kick or hit me when we disagreed. But there was one aspect of our agreement that I hadn't anticipated: the great relief I felt knowing that I wasn't going to resort to physical discipline anymore. Even though spankings had been a rarity, I had always felt guilty about them and knew spanking had somehow been a failure on my part. Seth had helped me to realize why."

Tom's story prompted David to recognize the link between his current treatment of his daughter and his childhood. "You know," he said, "if I'm really honest, I'd acknowledge that the times my dad hit me, I became enraged and thought he was unfair. I felt I didn't deserve such harsh punishment. The truth is, even though I adored my father and wanted to be like him, I wasn't very close to him. I was afraid of him and his temper."

David's adoration of his dad resulted from his longing to be close. Obviously, David's dad did not know that in order to protect and nourish the parent-child bond, he couldn't overwhelm and hurt his son whenever he was angry. We explained to David that by following guideline 1 of the Parenting Process he would disrupt his painful legacy and would be better able to establish a closeness with his daughter that had been impossible with his own father.

In our discussion, we could all trace Ann's school misbehavior back to her relationship with her dad. David had become a model for Ann's acting out. Because David hit when he was angry, he didn't show his daughter how to use more constructive behavior to resolve her angry feelings toward her classmates or him. Indeed, father and daughter had a strained relationship.

To complicate matters, Denise was unable to help her child. Her fears of conflict kept her from protecting Ann, which hurt her daughter's feelings and made Ann angry with Denise. Ann learned that she couldn't depend on Denise to keep her safe from her father.

So, in fact, Ann was emotionally abandoned by her mother while her father invaded her. Because the bond with her mom and dad was continually ruptured, Ann had no one to turn to. Moreover, she had no reliable source of safety and trust that would enable her to talk about her feelings or learn more appropriate ways to handle frustration.

Ann unconsciously justified her behavior at school because she was hit at home. If it was OK for dad to hit when he was angry, it must be OK for her. In fact, most of the kids in Ann's class were afraid of her. Consequently, she had trouble making and keeping friends. The inability to maintain closeness and intimacy in a relationship was handed down from David's father to David to Ann.

Healing the intimacy problem in this family began with a family meeting in our office in which we encouraged Denise and David to talk to Ann while keeping guideline 1 in mind. We supported Denise in being able to say to her husband in Ann's presence that spanking was inappropriate and was in fact exacerbating the problem. After several meetings with us, Ann began to see her mom as strong and supportive of her. She began to feel less abandoned.

We encouraged David to listen to Ann's emotions without argument. She told her dad, "It scares me when you hit me for hitting. You hurt me and my feelings. I don't like hitting my friends either, but I don't know what else to do when I get mad."

David began to understand that Ann needed help with this problem. Instead of being angry, he empathized with her. He, too, admitted he didn't know what to do when he became angry. David's own past and a lack of parenting skills were the cause of his frustration. Now, as David learned to be more empathic, Ann began to feel less invaded. The bonding that took place and the resulting safety and trust allowed this family to begin their search for real solutions.

If we punish our children for their misdeeds without investigating the feelings that underlie the behavior, we ignore the real problem. The first issue upon which to concentrate is the condition of the family's emotional bonds. Whenever you have a conflict with your kids, you must start at the beginning and examine whether you have unknowingly abandoned or invaded them.

Many times we invade or abandon our children subtly. We're lost in thought while they are talking to us; we yell at them from across the house without making direct contact; we ignore them or pretend to be listening to their stories. A constant stream of small injuries can add up. As adults, we need to remain aware of how our responses and behaviors might emotionally abandon or invade our children. If you are too preoccupied or exhausted to listen to your kids, you can say, "I'm too tired to listen right now. How about after dinner?" Just as small injuries add up, so do the good feelings that arise between our children and ourselves when we are attuned to each other.

Assessing Your Family's Bond

To assess the health of your family's bonds, ask yourself the following questions:

1. Do I make an effort to read and align with my child's emotional and physical states?
2. Am I physically affectionate with my children?
3. Do I accept my older children's needs for closeness?
4. Do I threaten to abandon my kids when they upset me?
5. Am I invasive and disrespectful of their feelings?
6. Do I become fragmented or withdraw when my children are upset with me?

When you stay in the present moment and do not parent in response to your past legacy, you will be less likely to invade or abandon your kids, thus creating safety, trust, and a strong bond. This satisfying relationship then becomes a model by which your children can establish and evaluate their present and future relationships.

6

Mirroring

Every child has a need to be noticed, understood, taken seriously, and respected.

Alice Miller, *Prisoners of Childhood*

The Parenting Process
Guideline 2: Mirror and Reflect Your Child's Feelings With Empathy

*E*mpathic attunement means the matching of your behavior to your child's emotional state. Your involvement nurtures emotional development, because as you listen to what your youngster tells you about his inner experience, you communicate your acceptance and validation.

Before we ever read about the theory and concept of empathic attunement, we learned by example how to tune into children from Molly Edmundson, a teacher with whom we trained at the Midtown School. The following is a sample of Molly's approach.

Ivan, a four-year-old in Molly's class, attended his first day of school wearing toy guns. The school, however, prohibited toy guns. Instead of taking the guns away, Molly told Ivan the rule. Then she added, "Since it's your first day you couldn't know about the rule beforehand. You can wear your guns this once, Ivan, but don't shoot at anyone. If the guns get too heavy, I'll put them where you can see them. They'll be safe there until it's time to go home."

When Ivan's mother, Diane, came to pick him up, Molly asked her privately about her son's interests.

"He likes to fix things and use tools," Diane replied.

The next day, Ivan wore his guns again, and Diane explained to Molly that he'd refused to leave home without them. Molly nodded. She took Ivan aside and said, "I see you still aren't ready to take off your guns. I understand. Ivan, come sit on the carpet with me. I have something to show you. Your mom told me you like to fix things. I brought some tools and this old radio that needs to be taken apart. Would you like to help me?"

Ivan was fascinated and soon asked Molly to help him remove his six-shooters because they were getting in his way. "Can you put them in the special place you told me about yesterday?" he wondered. Molly quickly obliged.

Soon several other children became intrigued by Molly and Ivan's activity. "Ivan is helping me fix this radio, and we could use more helpers," Molly explained. She was safely introducing Ivan into the life of the classroom, taking his own rhythm and interests into account. By using empathic attunement, Molly showed a deep respect for Ivan's personhood.

Empathic attunement is an attitude, a way of being with your children. When parents are empathic, they create an environment in which children can feel understood and accepted, an environment crucial for self-development. Parents can communicate this knowledge directly by using the verbal communication skill of *mir-*

roring their children's emotions. Empathy means responding to your child's inner life, and mirroring constitutes how you express that understanding. Through accurate mirroring, children know that they have successfully communicated their inner experience. Guideline 2 of the Parenting Process suggests that you *mirror and reflect your child's feelings with empathy.*

Cookie Battles—The Need for Mirroring

In one of our parenting classes, Barbara, a first-time mother, was having terrible power struggles with her three-year-old daughter, Allie. These conflicts made Barbara uncomfortable because they echoed her relationship with her mother, who was a strong, controlling woman. Barbara had always seemed to lose the fights she had with her mom.

In our class, the discussion focused on Barbara's struggles with Allie. Barbara told about an incident that occurred when she was wheeling her grocery cart slowly past the cookie section and Allie recognized a package of her favorite sweets. Surprising Barbara with her agility and quickness, the little girl grabbed the box and said, "Look, Mommy, my Oreos!"

"For a moment, I hesitated," Barbara reported. "I didn't really want to purchase the cookies. In fact, I'd been trying to cut down on Allie's intake of sweets. But I saw how excited my daughter was, and having been through such an episode before, I knew that refusing to buy the treat would trigger an argument, a big scene—right there in the middle of the aisle."

In the past, Barbara had periodically given in. But this time, she girded herself for the ensuing battle. "I forced myself to remain calm and hoped to handle this situation in a firm but civil fashion. 'Allie, you can't have those Oreos,' I told her. 'They're really not good for you.'

"Immediately, Allie's expression changed from excitement to hurt and then to anger and determination. Clinging tightly to the box, she stubbornly proclaimed, 'No!'"

Barbara tried to reason with her toddler as she became aware that people were watching. "Allie, I told you, these cookies have too much sugar," she reiterated. Yet such declarations made little impression on the resistant and independence-minded three-year-old, who responded with several increasingly firm, ear-splitting no's.

Feeling victimized and frustrated, much like she had as a little girl, Barbara started to lose control. In exasperation, she told her daughter, "Be a good girl," and demanded that Allie return the cookies immediately to avoid punishment.

Allie did not yield. Finally, unable to think of an alternative, Barbara grabbed her daughter's hand and pried the package loose from her tight grip. Allie began to scream uncontrollably. Then, feeling overwhelmed, embarrassed, and out of solutions, Barbara abandoned her shopping cart, picked up her wailing child and left the market for the privacy of her car. After fifteen minutes in the car, mother and daughter were finally able to calm down. Yet Barbara had the uneasy feeling that even though she had been victorious in the cookie battle, she was nevertheless losing the war. Barbara told us, "All the parenting books in the world just don't seem to help at a moment like this."

In order to handle situations such as these without overpowering a child physically or emotionally, it's essential to develop and use the skill of mirroring, in which you reflect your child's feelings.

Mirroring

Mirroring is the providing of an emotional reflection for your youngsters. In turning to you for validation, your children need to see themselves and identify their emotional experience. Just as you cannot see your face without looking into a mirror, your youngsters can't see who they are emotionally unless you provide them with an emotional looking glass. Your kids feel seen, heard, and understood when you reflect their experiences back to them. They are then better able to express their emotions and feel secure that you have accepted them.

Such expressions as "it sounds like," "it seems like," "what you're telling me is," and "what I hear you saying is," inform your children that you accurately understand their feelings.

Consider the situation in which your toddler begins to reach for a hot coffee pot. Obviously, it is necessary to stop her, yet it is difficult for her to resolve her anger at having her natural curiosity thwarted. When you reflect her anger back to her by using mirroring statements like "I know you want to touch the pot and you're angry that I won't let you. It's OK for you to be angry," you confirm her real emotional experience.

There is an important difference between "don't you get mad at me when I stop you from touching the pot" and "I can see how mad you are that I stopped you from touching the pot. It's OK to feel mad, but I'm still going to stop you because the coffee pot is too hot to touch." In the first instance you deny the child's reality, whereas in the second you validate it. Infants and toddlers begin to recognize their own emotions when parents clearly identify them and reflect them back with accurate mirroring. The toddler will experience a sense of "Yes! That's me. I'm mad, and the coffee pot is too hot!"

Barbara and Allie Resolve Their Conflict with Mirroring

If Barbara had known about mirroring, she might have realized that her daughter did not need to get her way as much as she needed her feelings acknowledged and mirrored. Her conflict with Allie might have been resolved like this:

Allie: Look, Mommy, my Oreos!

Barbara: I can see how excited you are. You really want them, don't you?

Allie: Yes, Mommy, my favorite cookies!

Barbara: You know what, Allie? Even though you're very excited, I don't want to buy them today. They have too much sugar. Put them back on the shelf.

Allie: No! No, I won't!

Barbara takes a deep breath in order to stay calm.

Barbara: I can see you want them, and I hear how mad you are. And you still have to put them back.

Allie: Sometimes you let me have them. I want them now!

Barbara: You're right, sometimes I do let you have them. It's really up to me to decide when it's a good time, and I know that this is not a good time.

Allie: I want the cookies! You're not fair. I don't like you!

Barbara: You're really mad at me right now, aren't you? You can be mad, *and* the Oreos still have to go back.

In this scenario, Barbara stays with Allie's feelings while she ignores the onlookers and keeps some emotional distance from Allie's comments, not taking them personally.

Allie has not totally capitulated, but she is beginning to give up the fight, because Barbara has not asked her to relinquish her right to *want* the cookies or to be *angry* with her mother for denying her request. She is entitled to her feelings even if her mother cannot fulfill her desires.

Allie: *(a trace of sadness replacing the angry tones):* "You put them back. I don't want to!"

Barbara: OK, I'll put them back for you. You're sad, and I can see that it's too hard for you to do it right now.

Mirroring and the Emerging Sense of Self

As we practice mirroring, our children begin to internalize their own separate and unique experience of themselves in the world. Many psychologists think of mirroring as providing the child with a picture of who he is. In their book *Body, Self, and Soul,* Drs. Jack Rosenberg and Marjorie Rand explain that mirroring "allows the child's self to continue expanding, and it gives him permission to be himself, to be different from his mother." It also permits children to have a distinct identity from their fathers!

When our youngster has frightening experiences, such as watching a scary television show, we often have difficulty remembering to mirror. We tend to deny or to suggest to her that she deny her fear. "It's just a story," we hear ourselves saying. When fears about fantasies like TV programs or nightmares occur, we commonly offer reassurances such as "Don't be scared. It's OK." A child feels more comforted, however, when you mirror his emotions. "You had a bad dream. You seem really scared. I'll sit next to you while you go back to sleep."

We all experience our emotions in our bodies. When children feel that their emotions have been affirmed, validated, and understood, integration and emotional release occurs. On the other hand, when children feel misunderstood, they continue to feel hurt and angry, and their sense of well-being diminishes. Without reflection and validation, kids literally hold their emotions in their bodies. They become emotionally contracted and closed. For example, everyone has seen a stubborn child. That stubbornness is reflected in the tightness of his jaw, the set expression in his face, and the muscle tension in his body. With accurate mirroring, children have the experience of releasing their emotions and recovering their sense of well-being.

We saw how this principle operates in our family when Seth was four and his Aunt Sylvia, with whom he was close, died. About four months after her death, Seth and Eileen were in the car on their way to do some errands. Seth turned to Eileen, with tears in his eyes and said, "Mom, I miss Aunt Syl." Eileen pulled the car over to the curb and began to mirror Seth. She put her arm around our son and said, "Seth, you really miss her, don't you? I see how sad you are." Seth's tears turned into sobs, which grew louder, reached a peak, and then subsided. In a few moments, the crying turned to deep sighs, and finally, after releasing his feelings, Seth turned to Eileen and said with dry eyes and a clear voice, "OK Mom, let's go to the store."

By accepting and reflecting your youngster's emerging self, you strengthen the parent-child bond. You communicate that the love between you endures, even as his separate self emerges. You're telling your youngster, "I'll be with you while you grow. I'll pay attention to what you tell me—with your words, with your body, and with your behavior. I will be present and will make every effort to understand your feelings and help you understand yourself. I will assist you with your difficulties without making you wrong. I'll make our relationship safe enough for you to risk expressing directly your authentic feelings." Mirroring is an act of love.

Clouding the Reflection

In many ways, we are what we feel. When a child's emotions are interrupted, frustrated, unacknowledged, or otherwise mirrored inaccurately, her budding sense of self is injured. If we ignore her hurt knee and then scold her for crying, she experiences the reprimand as a rejection and a denial of who she is. For children, these negative feelings can eventually accumulate into larger emotional experiences of shame, humiliation, and guilt, not only about what they do but more importantly, about who they are. Mirroring injuries are very common and get handed down from one generation to the next. Learning to mirror children's feelings is an important way to break the chain of emotional injuries.

But in order to reflect children's emotions accurately, we must present a mirror that is unclouded by our own confused emotions or our own legacies. When children look to us for mirroring they must receive a clear reflection of themselves and an equally clear sense of how we feel. In order to accurately mirror our children, we must become aware of our feelings as well as our biases. We need to be conscious of family patterns and the messages we have received and will be most likely to pass on (see chapters 2 and 3).

Our own emotions may get in the way of mirroring when kids engage in dangerous acts such as darting into traffic. Normally, parents experience a sharp pang of fear that may be masked by an overwhelming burst of anger in such stressful situations. Everyone's underlying emotions may get lost in the heat of our anger. Once *parents* can acknowledge their own fears, however, they become more available to precisely mirror their kids' feelings. An appropriate mirroring response to the child might be "When you ran into the street without looking, I got really scared, and that made me angry! It seems like you got scared, too, when the car honked its horn. We need to talk about how to cross the street so you can be safe and I don't have to worry."

Most of us have learned to deal with our kids' expressions of pain, anger, sadness, or upsetness by doing something—anything—to change the negative feeling to contentment. How many times have you seen a parent dangling a toy in front of a distressed toddler in order to distract her from being upset? Many parents believe that switching the focus makes a toddler feel better, when, in fact, too much distraction actually interferes with her opportunity to identify and master her own emotions. If you don't know how to reflect your child's feelings, you may resort to distraction to avoid confrontations. When used repeatedly as a technique or trick, however, distraction can become the mainstay of a parenting style. Thus, you may lose the opportunity to help your children with their emotional development.

Rather than distracting an upset child or chastising an angry one, through mirroring you create an emotional space that allows your youngsters to experience their hurt and then go on to other feelings, ideas, and alternatives. When we mirror our children, they gain emotional freedom and maneuvering room and learn to take control of their own feelings and behavior.

In our emotional life, there are no right or wrong feelings. Emotions have their own reality in the body. Many of us, however, have preconceived ideas, based on our family legacies, about which emotions are OK for children to feel and express. These biases reflect our comfort with our own feelings—which ones are acceptable for us to experience and which are not. By censoring certain feelings, we influence the outcome of our children's emotional development, since we interfere with their ability to stay in contact with those emotions. A parent who has difficulty handling anger may have a hard time tolerating anger in his children. This can result in youngsters who are reluctant to express their own anger or, conversely, who are angry all the time.

A father attending one of our workshops reported that at the age of four, he became very angry with his young and insecure mother. When he shouted, "I hate you!" at her, she collapsed in a heap of tears. Understandably, John became extremely frightened. The negative associations with anger remained with him. John was afraid of anger in himself and others. He traced his fear back to the episode with his mother. Her response led John to believe that his anger would destroy the people he loved and, conversely, that their anger would destroy him. Therefore, he shut his anger up inside. John was still stuck in the unresolved emotional dilemma he originally experienced with his mother. He lacked the flexibility to accept anger as a normal emotion.

We helped John understand that his difficulty with anger was handed down to him as a legacy and that he in turn might transmit this difficulty to his kids. We taught John to mirror his children's angry feelings even when those emotions made him feel uncomfortable. Mirroring would provide his youngsters the emotional room to experience and express their anger.

When mirroring is a part of family communication, our emotional bonds remain intact, even when we express our darker feelings, such as hurt and anger. When we trust that the bonds will not disintegrate from the force of our emotions, we create the opportunity to really work problems out, instead of covering up or suppressing our feelings. Such suppression and hiding can create emotional distance between parents and children.

Mirroring Injuries

Being able to recognize one's own feelings is an essential part of self-identity. Accurate mirroring brings about a child's acceptance of his feelings, which promotes his sense of self-worth and specialness. For example, Scott, an eighth grader, was chosen for a role in the school play. When he came home and told his father the news, Carl mirrored his son by saying, "I see how proud and excited you are that you were chosen."

Scott responded, "Yeah. I feel great."

Inaccurate mirroring, on the other hand, interferes with a child's authentic feelings, which is ultimately harmful to healthy development, self-esteem, and identity formation. Imagine three-year-old Vanessa, who falls down and merely looks at her knee. If we were frightened and anxious, we might say, "Oh my God, you hurt yourself!" That statement would be less an accurate reflection of Vanessa's emotional state than our own. Vanessa may become more upset to match our reaction or may act as if she were OK to calm us down. If, on the other hand, when Vanessa falls down and begins to wail, we respond by saying, "Get up, you're OK," we would deny her emotions too. In this case, Vanessa might hide her feelings, or her crying may intensify in her attempt to have us recognize her distress.

Accurate mirroring in the first instance would be a statement such as "Vanessa, I see you fell down. It seems like your knee hurts a little." In the second case, it would be, "Wow, you are crying hard. Sounds like you hurt yourself a lot."

Inaccurate mirroring creates mirroring injuries. There are several common mirroring injuries: undermirroring, overmirroring, distorted mirroring, and critical mirroring. Let's explore these in more detail.

Undermirroring

Undermirroring occurs when you respond with less emotional intensity than your child expresses. For example, Jonathan tells you that he is very excited about the upcoming school fair. His voice is high-pitched and bubbly, and he can barely contain himself. Your response, however, is flat. You barely acknowledge your child's excitement. As a result, Jonathan feels invisible or unimportant. He might believe his feelings don't matter or that something is wrong with his excitement.

Overmirroring

Overmirroring occurs when the reflection you provide your children is an exaggeration of their feelings or accomplishments. For example, Audrey may say that she likes the painting she just made. You respond with, "That's the best painting I've ever seen, I bet you're going to be a famous artist. When are you going to have your own show?" Audrey would feel mistrust, and her real accomplishment would be diminished.

Distorted Mirroring

Distorted mirroring occurs when your response has no connection to the feelings your child expresses. If Linda comes home and tells you she has just made the debate team, and you answer by asking her when she is going to clean her room, then Linda cannot see herself in your response, and consequently she would feel unimportant and alone.

Critical Mirroring

When you mirror critically, you discount the feelings your child presents. You may be overtly critical, as in "That is a stupid way to feel," or well-intentioned, responding, for example, "Don't be silly, everyone likes you" when Robert complains that he has no friends. Critical mirroring makes children doubt they are entitled to their emotions. They feel wrong and bad.

Exaggeration or Reality?

Sometimes parents have trouble mirroring their children's feelings because they decide that these emotions are exaggerated or faked. Years ago, when Eileen was a nursery school teacher, a four-year-old in her group told his dad he was afraid there were lions in his closet. The father insisted that his son accept the reality that there were no lions in the closet. This was true enough, but we all know that when we're scared and someone says, "Don't be frightened," the advice seldom helps.

What the father neglected to do was to make an empathic connection with his son through mirroring. Dad could have said, "You are really feeling afraid that there are lions in the closet, aren't you? I know a lion cannot live in there. Why don't you hold my hand and we'll look together."

Children often use images and fantasy to convey important emotional states. Mirroring allows your child to identify and locate his feelings inside, thus beginning to clarify the difference between himself and others. Without your empathic bond such openness is impossible. This is why it's essential that you refrain from arbitrarily deciding that your child's feelings are *mere* exaggeration.

How Mirroring Defuses Power Struggles

Janet and Steve participated in a series of workshops and reported back to us on how mirroring had changed their relationship with their daughter. The couple enjoyed their parenting role and were loving and conscientious. Janet and Steve shared a common legacy from their respective families. They were told to feel good and be happy all the time. They complained of few problems within their family except frequent power struggles with their preschooler. Three or four times a week their four-year-old, Caroline, whined all the way home from school about her "yucky" day. Janet and Steve responded by encouraging their daughter to focus on positive events during the school day. Caroline resisted their attempts to change her feelings and would reiterate that nothing good had happened. That was the trigger for the power struggle. The more Mom and Dad suggested the fun Caroline might have had or coaxed her into optimism, the more she complained about how awful school had been.

We taught Janet and Steve about mirroring, and in a follow-up interview, they related a story about how their relationship with Caroline had improved. The next time Steve picked up their preschooler, the conversation proceeded as follows:

Steve: How was school today, Caroline?

Caroline: Terrible. I hate school, and Jenny's not my friend.

Steve: Sounds like you had a bad day at school. What happened between you and Jenny?

Caroline: Jenny wouldn't eat lunch with me. She played with Amy, and now she's her friend, not mine.

Steve: Seems like you're sad about that, like your feelings are hurt. No wonder you're telling me you hate school.

Caroline: Yeah. She did hurt my feelings.

Steve: It hurts to feel left out. Did anything else happen at school today that you didn't like?

Caroline: My clay doggy that was drying on the shelf got knocked over when Billy and Josh were fighting, and it broke.

Steve: No wonder you're upset. That's two hard things that happened today.

Caroline: But Monica, my teacher, helped me glue the legs back on, and she said I could paint it tomorrow.

Steve: You sound excited about that.

Caroline: I am. I'm going to paint him yellow!

At first Steve was tempted to come to Caroline's aid by suggesting more positive aspects of her day, as he usually did. But this time he held back and mirrored her feelings instead. He didn't try to discount her evaluation of her day. Before the conversation ended, Steve saw that once he mirrored Caroline's negative feelings, she began to shift on her own. She became more positive because she wasn't forced to conform to Steve's expectations. Caroline's more positive attitude grew spontaneously, much to her dad's surprise and delight. And as Caroline felt Steve accept her emotions, she no longer needed to defend them as stubbornly. The old power struggle lost its potency. Now Caroline was free to share her excitement with her dad.

Within every power struggle resides our desire to have our feelings recognized and understood by the other. The underlying struggle, then, is not over the content of our arguments, but rather over our desire that our opponent sees, hears, understands, and accepts our feelings.

When we mirror, we create the emotional space for differences of opinion, feelings, and perceptions. When your children perceive that you understand their position and feelings, their need to fight dissolves. Then conflict resolution can replace the power struggle.

Besides, it is easy for you to psychologically or intellectually overpower your child, even if he's a teenager. And power struggles are never won; they continue to play out over and over again, even though the content may change. In fact, power struggles between teenagers and parents are common. Here, too, mirroring works wonders.

Resolving Power Struggles with Teens

Joey and his dad, Hank, came to see us at the suggestion of Joey's high-school counselor. Joey was a bright and lively 16-year-old. A junior in high school, he played guard on the basketball team. He was well liked, had a girlfriend, and got along well with his teachers. Joey's grades were generally good, although he was having trouble with math, in which he barely maintained a C-minus average. Joey always seemed to leave his math book at school, and even when he did manage to complete a homework assignment, he often left it at home.

Hank, a strong-willed father whose own dad had had high expectations of him, believed that Joey should keep all of his grades at B or better. This C-minus was unacceptable. He had laid down the law: Until the math grade improved, Joey's weekend curfew would be cut back from 1:00 A.M. to 11:00 P.M. No more late parties. Period!

Lately, father and son seemed to repeat the same argument every Friday night. Joey complained to his father that he was being unfair. "All my friends are allowed to stay out later. You treat me like a child! My other grades are OK."

Unfortunately, Joey's insistence merely hardened his father's resolve. "I don't care about everybody else. You are going to toe the line," Hank answered "Until you bring your math grade up, you're coming home at eleven. And if you keep arguing with me, you're not going out at all!"

Joey felt angry, frustrated, and powerless. Usually he delivered a parting shot—"I'm never going to bring my math grade up. I hope I flunk the dumb class"—before storming out the door.

Father and son were at a standoff. The arguments hadn't inspired Joey to improve his math. The legacy of dealing with high expectations without support for the difficulties one might naturally experience in the process of learning had caused Joey to avoid mastering those subjects that came hard to him. Joey rationalized his poor math grade as acceptable since he was doing well in everything else. He felt his father was rigid and arbitrary, and he saw no connection between a weekend curfew and improvement in math.

Hank, for his part, had no sense of why Joey was experiencing so much trouble with math. He had no idea what kind of support Joey might need. He hadn't determined if Joey's resistance was simply spiteful behavior, an attempt to establish independence in an unproductive way, or some other issue he hadn't considered.

It was clear to us that neither Joey nor his dad understood how to listen to each other. There was some truth in each one's position, but since they both lacked the ability to mirror each other, neither felt properly seen or heard.

When working with Joey and Hank, we taught them the importance of reflecting each other's feelings *before* asserting one's own position.

We modeled mirroring for them:

Tom:	Joey, it sounds as if you're hurt and angry, and you feel as if your dad is way off base.
Joey:	Yeah, that's right. He never listens, he doesn't care.
Tom:	So when he enforces this curfew, you feel uncared for?
Joey:	Yeah.
Eileen	(to Hank:) Joey's telling you he feels uncared for. Do you care about him?
Hank:	Hell, yes! That's why I'm doing this. You know, when one grade slips, they all slip, and pretty soon his life's a mess. He won't be able to get a scholarship, and we can't afford to pay the full cost of his college education.
Eileen:	You're expressing your love for Joey by making this rule? You feel concerned about his future?

Hank:	Yes.
Tom:	Joey, your dad says he cares about you and that's why he's being so strict.
Joey:	It doesn't feel that way. He puts me under so much pressure. When I feel pressured, it just makes me not want to study my math. Seems like my dad only cares about my grade and not about me.
Eileen:	Joey is saying again that he feels pressure and that he doesn't feel cared for, like the good things he is doing aren't good enough.
Hank:	Sure, they're good enough. But I am pressuring him. How else is he going to learn to apply himself to things he doesn't do well?
Joey:	That just makes it worse! If you think you're helping, you aren't.
Hank:	I don't know what else to do.
Tom:	You sound frustrated and helpless, Hank, as if you don't know how to help him. Have you asked Joey why he feels like he's having such a hard time in math?

Hank hung his head and admitted that he had not asked.

Hank:	I thought it was just because he was being rebellious about curfew or that he wasn't applying himself. I felt I couldn't give in. I believe it's important for teenagers to have rules and not to have wishy-washy parents.
Eileen:	So your way to help is to be tough and not give in?
Hank:	That's right.
Tom:	Well, let's hear from Joey what's going on in math class. Why do you think you're having problems, Joey?

Joey: The concepts are hard, and I feel kind of
          stupid. I'm smart enough in my other classes,
          so I just turned my back on this class. I don't
          like feeling dumb.

We pointed out to Joey and Hank that by mirroring
both of them, we all had more information now. Hank
learned that his son was avoiding math because the difficulty of mastering the concepts made him feel bad
about himself. Joey learned that his dad's intention was
to help him and not let him down. We encouraged father
and son to continue the dialogue, mirroring as they went
on.

Hank: So the real problem is that you feel bad about
          yourself because of the trouble you're having
          in math?

Joey: That's right. And you. You're concerned about
          me, that maybe I won't get a scholarship if
          my math grade doesn't improve.

Hank: Yeah. I'm anxious because this isn't the same
          kind of math that I learned in school so I can't
          help you. I don't like not being able to help
          you. It makes *me* feel stupid. I guess
          realistically, though, I'm not the right one to
          help. Can you find a tutor or spend some time
          after class with your teacher?

Joey: A bunch of the seniors act as tutors during
          lunch. I guess I could ask one of them. But
          what about the curfew?

Hank: When I see that you're willing to do
          something positive to help yourself, it makes
          me willing to let go of the curfew as a way to
          pressure you. Tell you what, if you get a
          tutor and put in extra time on your math, I'll
          let you go back to the 1:00 A.M. limit on the
          weekends.

With mirroring, Joey and his dad discovered the real problem and found some workable solutions. Joey felt supported for what he was feeling, not merely criticized for his performance, and Hank felt that his real concerns were understood. This changed the mirroring injury that was Hank's legacy from his father. Now Hank supported Joey in a learning process, instead of just expecting him to perform. Moreover, Joey's experience of feeling misunderstood by his father had driven a wedge between them. Learning how to mirror allowed them to feel closer, thus strengthening their bond.

Adolescence is a difficult time. Teenagers pass through a wide range of feelings and moods on any given day. Understanding your teens' emotional life can be frustrating because one moment they expect you to take care of them and the next moment they seem to push you away, demanding that they be treated like an adult. Remember, teens are in the process of forging separate identities. Mirroring supports a feeling of acceptance, no matter what their emotions happen to be at any given moment. Mirroring also allows your teens the freedom to move between closeness and separateness.

Assessing Your Mirroring Skills

To assess your mirroring skills, answer the following questions:

1. Do I recognize and reflect my children's emotions even when their feelings make me uncomfortable?

2. Do I interrupt, frustrate, ignore, or deny my children's feelings?

3. Do I allow my own emotional legacy to cloud my children's image of themselves?

4. Can I acknowledge my own feelings?

5. Do I try to distract my children from their upset feelings or chastise them when they are angry?

6. Do I undermirror or overmirror?

7. Do I mirror distortedly or critically?

Any new skill takes time and practice to develop. At first mirroring may feel mechanical. However, there is a difference between automatically parroting back your children's words and taking the time to put yourself in their emotional shoes—finding the words to describe your sense of their experience. If you mirror mechanically, your children will feel the disparity between authentic empathy and empty words that are supposed to express emotional understanding. When you mirror from your heart, rather than from your intellect, you will feel the difference. And so will your kids.

7

Separation

As a child separates he will learn the conditions of actual love and acquire the sense that he is himself and nobody else.

Louise Kaplan, *Oneness and Separateness*

The Parenting Process

Guideline 3: Remember Your Child Is Separate from You, with Separate Thoughts and Feelings.

Don, a member of one of Tom's men's groups, is an athletic and active father. His father, on the other hand, a salesman who had traveled often, had been an uninvolved parent. When Anthony was born, Don had promised himself that he would change this legacy. When Anthony entered junior high school, on weekends Don made a point of playing football with him and he was proud of the fact that he had never missed one of Anthony's football games.

One day during his junior year of high school, however, Anthony came to Don and said, "Dad, I've decided drop football next fall. I'm going to try out for the school play."

Don was disappointed. "You're going to give up your spot on the team to be in the play?"

"You know I have fun with football," Anthony replied, "but I've always wanted to try acting, and this is my chance."

Don felt upset, because football was an activity they had always enjoyed together. Don was aware that to a great extent, his reaction was colored by the disappointment he had felt as a child because his father hadn't been involved in his activities. He understood, however, that his disappointment was separate from his son's true interest.

"I'll miss helping you with football," Don said, "but I really do want you to pursue your own interests."

Anthony was relieved that his dad supported him. He felt that Don was really on his side. "You know, Dad," he said, "I'm going to need help learning my lines for the audition. Would you help me?"

Because Don identified the real source of his disappointment, he didn't force his son to continue playing football in order to cement their ties or make up for the closeness he had missed with his father. In fact, when Don maintained an awareness of his legacy, he could remain emotionally separate from Anthony, which enhanced their authentic closeness. Don adhered to the third guideline of the Parenting Process. He remembered that his child was separate from him with separate thoughts and feelings. Paradoxically, closeness has a greater opportunity to develop when parents acknowledge their separateness.

What is Separation?

After infants are born, their first experience of life is one of separation. When the umbilical cord is cut, your baby starts his unique journey through life.

Psychologically, separation is a process in which your children emotionally differentiate themselves from you. In order to accomplish this, they must have your understanding, support, and acknowledgment of their independence and autonomy.

Separation means that boundaries clearly define each person in the relationship. You and your children have distinct emotional experiences in which you are allowed your own thoughts and feelings. There is room in the relationship for emotional differences.

You may fear emotional separation because you imagine it involves one or more of the following consequences:

- Losing your relationship with your children.
- Being disconnected.
- Being alone or lonely.
- Your children always getting their way.
- Prematurely throwing your children out of the nest to fend for themselves.

Actually, separation is none of these things. As we'll explain, it is essential for developing close relationships with your children. Indeed, healthy and authentic separation is the third and final step of the Parenting Process.

Using guideline 3 will help you establish and maintain your children's sense of self and free them from your unresolved emotional legacy. Separation, just like bonding and mirroring, is an ongoing developmental theme.

Why Separation and Boundaries Are Important

Each family member is a living system—a set of interacting units—that processes matter, energy, or information. A boundary outlines and defines the system, allowing it to develop internal order despite a continually changing environment.

When your children have a sense of their own psychological or emotional boundaries, they can identify who they are as distinct from you or others. Their boundaries allow them to let in love, support, and affection. Boundaries support a sense of the individual's identity in the family environment, so that your youngsters feel worthwhile, even when they encounter your upsetness, anger, or fragmentation.

An emotional boundary creates the opportunity for your kids to balance and move between their needs for oneness and intimacy on the one hand and separateness and autonomy on the other. Without authentic, clearly defined separateness from our children, we risk having an enmeshed, smothering relationship, a distant one that lacks warmth, or one that swings between both extremes.

Boundaries are equally important for parents. When our children are upset or critical of us, we must maintain our boundaries in order to feel adequate as parents. As we maintain our emotional boundaries, we can listen to our children's critical feelings, consider those feelings, and respond to them appropriately.

For example, Josie told her eight-year-old son, Blake, that he had to pick up his toys before he could play Nintendo.

Blake was really angry. "You are the meanest mom there is!" he said.

Josie maintained her boundaries. She knew her request was reasonable. She didn't personalize Blake's anger by reacting angrily and defending herself. Rather, she mirrored his feelings by saying, "Wow. You are really angry!"

In addition, when we have clearly defined boundaries, we are more aware of our emotional legacies. We can identify these injuries and longings and refrain from assigning them to our children.

Foremost, we experience our boundaries in our bodies. Because we sense feelings internally, our emotional boundary is a physical experience. Boundaries are a sort of emotional skin. Actually, real skin functions in much the same way. First, it defines each of us as separate individuals. Second, it is permeable, constantly allowing for the exchange of oxygen, water, and energy in a rhythmic give-and-take with the environment. These two qualities—separation and contact—are what we need psychologically. Our real skin and our emotional skin differ, however, in that while the former is tangible, the latter is felt only by each individual and is invisible to the outside world.

It is our task to help our children identify their feelings. When your kids articulate their individual emotional experience, how they think or feel, what they need or want, this expression becomes a boundary. When you allow your youngsters to directly express their authentic experience, they are then able to define who they are within the family. With appropriate boundaries, relationships with your children can be warm, intimate, and supportive.

How to Establish Appropriate Boundaries

In order for authentic separation and boundary formation to occur, you must remember to incorporate all three Parenting Process guidelines:

- Protect the bond.
- Mirror your children's feelings.
- Respect your children's unique experience.

Separation is an ongoing, lifelong process. It is both a concept and a part of your relationship with your kids. In addition to keeping your children's separate identity in mind, it is helpful when expressing your own thoughts and feelings to use "I" statements.

Using "I" Statements

"I" statements contain the word I rather than you. When we use "I" statements to communicate our thoughts and feelings to our children, we convey *our* emotional experience, rather than theirs. For example, saying "You slob. Clean up your room" is critical and likely to produce a defensive reaction. It is a description of the child's behavior rather the parent's response to the behavior. The use of an "I" message, such as "I'm not happy with all your clothes on the floor. I'd like you to pick them up," does not injure the child's self-esteem. "I" statements allow nonjudgmental interactions that provide room for differing feelings and opinions. A respectful encounter occurs. "I" statements model separateness. Rather than telling children who they are and how they *should* feel and think, they create exchanges between family members in which emotional information is shared.

Walter, an executive of a large company, wanted to use "I" messages to his family's advantage. Walter attended one of our workshops at the suggestion of his wife, who was concerned that he was ordering their daughters around, treating them like employees rather than kids.

During our discussion of separation, Walter shared an important realization. "I've been agonizing over whether to change my daughter Carrie's tennis teacher. I've been writing a list of pros and cons and asking friends for recommendations. She's a talented player, so I want her to have the best instruction. But I just realized that I never discussed changing teachers with her. I've been exploring this issue independently. I have no idea how she feels about her current teacher."

The next day Walter returned to the workshop, excited to share the outcome of his new learning. "I talked to my daughter, Carrie, last night," he explained. Instead of telling her *she* should change her teacher, I told her *I* had been questioning whether or not her teacher was still adequate. I wanted to know her opinion."

"Carrie said, 'You know, Dad, that's funny, because I've been thinking about the same thing too. I'm really glad you asked me. I like my teacher, and I still think she has a lot to teach me, but I want to go to a tennis clinic this summer to experience some other coaching as well.' "

Walter was relieved. He had avoided a power struggle and refrained from treating his daughter like an employee by making decisions for her. Using "I" statements, Walter was able to appreciate Carrie as a separate person with her own boundaries and needs. Walter's new awareness enhanced their opportunity for closeness.

Sometimes parents can be aware of problems in separation and still have difficulty in changing their ingrained patterns. We recommend the following steps to help with boundary difficulties:

1. Use Guideline 3 to monitor your interactions with your children, noticing if you allow your kids to have thoughts and feelings distinct from yours.

2. Mirror your youngsters' separate thoughts and feelings.

3. Use "I" statements to communicate your own separate thoughts and feelings.

When Boundaries Are Too Vague

When parental boundaries are undefined, you may risk identifying too closely with your children. You may have difficulty recognizing the difference between your feelings and your children's. For instance, a parent with undefined boundaries might assume that if he is cold or hungry, his child is also cold or hungry.

Youngsters, in turn, will be unable to distinguish where their sense of self begins or ends if their boundaries are unclear. They may have difficulty locating an internal reference point because they haven't developed a sense of being the author of their own actions. When boundaries are undefined, youngsters lose their center of initiative and well-being. They may feel forced to comply with their parents' emotional reality. For example, the child whose parent assumes she is cold and hungry may accept a sweater or food even when she is not cold or hungry. Because she lacks practice, this child may eventually have difficulty in learning how to identify her own needs.

Unfortunately, when boundaries are vague, children may feel pressed to choose between the relationship with their parents and their authentic experience. Most often, they will accommodate the relationship because of their physical and emotional dependence, yet when youngsters suppress their emotions out of compliance, their feelings will remain unattended to and unresolved. Without firm boundaries, children will not have learned how to have both themselves and their relationships.

Kaye, a mother with whom we worked, was a frustrated actress. We saw her in our office along with her teenage daughter, Lilly. Kaye had given up her dream of an acting career to raise her family. She wanted Lilly to have the life she had never achieved. Kaye had lost her boundaries with her daughter and was unaware of the difference between them. From the time Lilly was a toddler, Kaye enrolled her in acting classes and beauty pageants. She even auditioned Lilly for television commercials.

As a little girl, Lilly learned to please her mother by pursuing acting. She never developed interests outside of those her mother wanted for her. This was her way of trying to be close to her mother. Consequently, Lilly became a classic people pleaser in her relationships with her mom as well as her teenage friends. Because separation hadn't occurred between Lilly and her mother, Lilly never learned how to convey her authentic needs and desires in relationships. No matter how many people she befriended, she never felt satisfied. She remained filled with longing for closeness but lacked the separate sense of self that is required to create true intimacy.

As we helped Kaye and Lilly become aware of the boundary issues between them, mother and daughter felt permission to have their own separate interests. Kaye had the emotional room to grieve about her lost career. Lilly started to feel that her life was her own and stopped trying to please her mother.

When Boundaries Are Too Rigid

When parents' boundaries are rigid and inflexible, children may lack the emotional contact they need to feel intimate and close. In addition, when parents' boundaries are rigid, children grow up too quickly and become responsible beyond their years. Emotional separation occurs prematurely, and kids are forced to function beyond their developmental reach. These children are pushed into adult roles while they still have childhood dependency needs. A father with rigid boundaries, for example, might expect his three-year-old son to get his own breakfast. And if his son complained, he might say, "You have to learn to be a big boy."

Adults who have had to grow up too quickly feel as if they've missed their childhood. Never allowed to be children, they learned instead to be strong, tough, and competent, and to hold themselves together in adversity. It is difficult for such people to feel or show their neediness and vulnerability. It also becomes difficult for them to tolerate needy, vulnerable feelings in others, including their own children. Such parents become easily frustrated and angry when faced with their children's developmental limitations.

Intimacy and closeness must include the ability to allow another person to see those parts of yourself that are disorganized, incompetent, and weak. When you require your kids to be little adults, your relationship with them will lack warmth, compassion, and understanding. Your children, in turn, may experience their relationship with you as distant, even if it's caring. When children grow up with parents who have uncompromising or unyielding boundaries, they have no model for closeness that includes warmth and tenderness. Later, in adult life, these independent children often have difficulty creating intimacy.

Brenda and Jake, successful attorneys and self-assured parents, came to our workshop because they believed, as they put it, "You can never be too competent." They were proud of their five-year-old son, Alan. As Jake explained, "Alan is such a grown-up little man that most of the time he hardly seems to need us. But every once in a while, when he comes home from school, Alan falls apart like he is a two-year-old. We really don't understand why this happens and whether we should be concerned."

We asked these parents to describe a typical incident. "Yesterday, I picked up Alan at five o'clock from after-school care," Brenda reported. "I told him to put away his things and set the table, which is his usual job. When he started whining, I reminded him that big boys don't whine and that he had better stop. He got more upset, and I sent him to his room. He had a tantrum and tore up all the pictures he had drawn at school yesterday."

We advised Jake and Brenda that at the age of five, Alan was still a little boy. It was natural for him to have a hard time being responsible so close to dinnertime, especially after a long day at school. Their expectations of him were unrealistically high. We suggested to these parents that they had separated themselves from their son too severely. Upon coming home from school, Alan needed their affection and warmth and not just instructions. For Brenda and Jake, guideline 3 meant tuning in to Alan's separate five-year-old experience, rather than their adult expectations.

Brenda and Jake's willingness to learn how to be more emotionally involved softened the strict and stiff boundaries between them and their son. As a result of their adopting guideline 3, Alan could begin to experience a relationship in which his parents modeled warmth and closeness for him.

When Boundaries Alternate Between Being Vague and Rigid

Most parents' boundaries are by turns ambiguous and unyielding, and consequently parents are alternately too involved with their kids and then not involved enough. At times they themselves expect their children to be extensions of themselves, thinking and feeling exactly as they do; at other times, they are distant and uncompromising in an attempt to help their children grow up.

Children have three basic responses to this boundary confusion. They may become compliant, they may rebel, or they may combine both reactions and become passive-aggressive.

Children who comply tend to be the good boys and good girls that we described in chapter 2. Compliant children do what they are told in order to secure the bond with their parents. They don't have an internalized sense of self, because they experience separation as an emotional risk. It threatens the bond between them and their parents. The message their parents send is "Don't be different from me." Therefore, compliant children tend to be anxious about emotional abandonment.

Joni, a worried mother in one of our workshops, had an eight-year-old daughter, Kate. She was anxious about letting her child spend the night away from home. Because Kate was compliant, she never asked Joni to let her sleep at her girlfriend's, even though she wanted to do so. Kate was afraid to let her mother know her real feelings, because they were different from Joni's.

Children who rebel place themselves in opposition to their parents in an attempt to maintain some small portion of a separate identity. These kids continually lock into bouts of spitefulness, stubbornness, and contrariness with their parents. If you say, "Let's go," they want to stay. If you say, "Put on your shoes," they want to go barefoot. The result is a never-ending cycle of power struggles. Rebellious children feel as if they are backed into a corner and must fight to establish enough psychological room to have their own identity. However, when children adopt this behavior pattern, their identity, too, is inauthentic. It emanates solely from being in opposition. They only know who they are when they react; they don't really know how they feel. For example, Todd refused to follow any directions his teacher gave him and was often sent to the principal's office. Todd learned a pattern of rebelling against authority because at home his parents did not give him the emotional room to have his own feelings. They continually told him what to do and how to feel, so he continued to feel and do the opposite.

Children may also adapt to their parents' alternating boundaries by using passive-aggressive behavior. Passive-aggressive children vacillate between compliance and rebellion. They look as if they are being a "good girl" or a "good boy" and will agree to parents' demands, but they make commitments and promises which they never seem to fulfill. Passive-aggressive kids appear to comply but in truth rebel. They say, in effect, "I don't know what my own needs are, but I know I don't want to do what you say!" Eileen recognizes this response in her own behavior toward her father. Every time Eileen left the house, for instance, her dad hollered, "Wear your jacket!"

Eileen would put on her jacket, appearing to respond, yet as soon as she got down the block, she removed it. "I'd rather be cold than do what he says!" she thought. As a young girl, Eileen paid more attention to reacting to her father's command than she did to her own feelings of comfort.

How to Interrupt the Transmission of Boundary Problems

Boundary problems are transmitted from one generation to the next because boundaries are a fundamental aspect of the sense of self. They determine how we structure our relationships. With strong, clear boundaries, we are able to be intimate with another person while maintaining our feelings of independence. It is inevitable that the boundary issues we first experience with our parents will resurface with our children because we are so deeply interrelated emotionally, psychologically, and biologically.

In looking at our family history, it is important to identify our parents' boundary style. Using the questionnaire, tracking your own fragmentation, and keeping a parenting journal (see chapter 3) will help you become more familiar with your own legacy. As you become aware of your boundary style, monitor your interactions with your kids using guideline 3, mirror your youngsters' thoughts and feelings, and use "I" statements to help interrupt your legacy.

In addition, you can begin to notice whether you are uncomfortable with your children's need for closeness, their need for autonomy, or both. This will allow you to diagnose your own boundary issues.

Guideline 3 is a way to break the chain of boundary problems that reach back for generations. When you understand and use the guideline for separation, you can establish and respect your children's boundaries.

Then your youngsters will have both their independence and a sense of closeness within the family.

Separation and Sex-Role Development

As children deal with the theme of separation, they not only identify themselves as separate and unique beings, but they also learn who they are as members of their particular gender. There are important differences in the separation process for little boys and little girls. These differences affect children's future development.

When mothers are the only primary care givers, they also become the principle receivers of their child's earliest and deepest joys as well as his earliest frustrations and rages. As Dorothy Dinnerstein, author of *The Mermaid and the Minotaur,* explains, "For the girl as well as the boy, a woman is the first center of bodily comfort and pleasure, and the first being to provide the vital delight of social intercourse. The initial experience of dependence on a largely uncontrollable outside source of good is focused on a woman, and so is the earliest experience of vulnerability, of disappointment, and pain."

For the developing infant, the longing to merge with mother and the desire to move away and develop autonomy are simultaneous and conflicting emotional drives. The comfort of merging and fusing with mother can be experienced as dangerous to that part of the child that is moving toward separateness. Conversely, the movement toward independence can threaten the need for intimacy.

Since mothers historically have been the primary care-givers, young children deal with separation by first distinguishing their own identities from their mothers'. In general, girls learn the difference between themselves and their mothers in a context of sameness, because they are both female. In contrast, boys learn to distinguish their identity in a context of differentness, because they are male. These disparities affect a child's sense of self.

According to Nancy Chodorow, author of *The Reproduction of Mothering,* when a girl realizes she is separate from her mother, she does not have to deny those qualities in herself that are mother-like and therefore female, such as emotional connectedness, warmth, and tenderness. As a little boy separates from his mother, however, he begins to identify himself with his father (or another masculine figure) and must divorce himself from his mother in a significantly more rigid manner. In order to feel like a boy, he cannot identify with "female" qualities. This disparity in separation patterns sets the stage in the psyche of boys and girls for the vast gender differences that are perpetuated by the legacies of individual families and the culture at large.

These differences affect children in many ways. In her book *In a Different Voice,* psychologist Carol Gilligan explains that these distinctions influence how children develop morally and how they perceive problems. When solving a problem, for instance, a girl might consider the maintenance of the relationship as the most important issue. A boy, on the other hand, might emphasize the ethical dimension of a decision, without considering the relationship. Consequently, it is still common for women to be thought of as less capable of making hard, tough decisions. Gender prejudices such as "girls can't be strong" and "boys can't be emotional" may result from a lack of understanding of the developmental differences that occur when boys and girls separate from their mothers. In addition, girls' moral development is judged in relation to the development of boys' and is not equally valued. Gender prejudices are transmitted as part of a child's emotional legacy.

One important way to balance these developmental differences is for fathers to be intimately and actively involved in the care and raising of infants and young children. When fathers as well as mothers nurture children, both boys and girls will have permission to be warm and tender and strong and independent.

Assessing Your Separation Skills

To assess your separation skills, ask yourself the following questions:

1. Do I recognize that my child is a separate person with his own thoughts and feelings?

2. Do I maintain my own boundaries in spite of my child's disapproval?

3. Do I help my child identify his own feelings?

4. Do I use "I" statements to communicate my feelings?

5. Are my boundaries vague or rigid?

6. Do I restrict my child's emotional development because of his or her gender?

In the next chapter, you will see how the three guidelines, when used together as a single process, offer a way to interrupt and alter the emotional legacies that restrict and interfere with your children's unique development. The Parenting Process facilitates the movement between family closeness and individual independence.

8

A New Way of Relating: The Parenting Process in Action

Human history becomes more and more a race between education and catastrophe . . . the past is but a beginning of a beginning, and all that is and has been is but the twilight of the dawn. A day will come when beings who are now latent in our thoughts and hidden in our loins shall stand upon this earth as one stands upon a footstool and shall laugh and reach out their hands amid the stars.

H. G. Wells, *The Open Conspiracy: Blueprints for a World Revolution*

*C*urrents of emotion continually shift in families. We experience times of love, acceptance, and special closeness as well as moments when hurt and anger bring pain and when differences and emotional gulfs seem almost too wide to bridge. During the difficult times, it is important to remember that we all become emotionally injured when we feel unaccepted or misunderstood. But it is comforting to note that distressing situations are also opportunities for families to establish a feeling of intimacy and caring.

A reassuring closeness comes from resolving conflicts fairly, equitably, and with respect for individual differences. Of course, it is easy for us to talk about patching up differences and solving family disputes, but in the heat of anger how do you step back from the intensity of the hurt to identify the moment as part of life rather than an abnormal event? The answer is to apply the Parenting Process to your family's unique problems.

Resolving Conflicts: Using the Three Guidelines

When Seth was nine, he took piano lessons, at his own request. At one point, Tom noticed that Seth had become reluctant to practice, and when he did, he was easily frustrated and finished early. Tom was also aware that watching Seth's struggle stirred up his old memories of wanting to quit when he became frustrated while learning to play. He had also felt alone and unsupported in this struggle when he was a boy.

If Tom had remained unconscious of his own unresolved emotions, he might have said to Seth, "Listen, you have to learn to overcome your frustrations, so you must practice the piano. The only way you're going to learn is if I make you. I'm setting the rule—you are not quitting your lessons. I think piano is important, and you are going to learn."

Instead, Tom decided to use his parenting journal first (see chapter 3). His entry read:

"Seth doesn't want to practice because he feels defeated. On a scale of 1 to 10, this upsets me at about an

8. I know if I approach him as upset as I am now, we will never get anywhere, so I'd better wait and see what part of my own legacy has become activated. I remember feeling frustrated, defeated, and alone when I was learning music. I decided I couldn't do it. My father kept telling me that no one in our family had musical talent, so I was reluctant to ask for help and support. I was afraid he was right. This made it difficult to enjoy the process of learning and to allow myself to be a beginner. Now I experience these same feelings as I observe Seth's struggle. I'm afraid that somehow Seth is also going to feel discouraged unless I force him to practice. But when I really think about what I needed then, it wasn't more rules. I wish my parents could have helped me understand that I wasn't dumb and that music was sometimes difficult to learn. Making mistakes is a part of learning. I wish that they could have encouraged me to stick with it."

After Tom reread this journal entry, he felt calmer and clearer about his own emotional issues and more separate from Seth. He was aware of his boundary and could distinguish between his own experience in the past and Seth's current problem. The next time Seth had difficulty with the piano, Tom anticipated that he would be able to help him.

The opportunity arose soon enough. One especially discouraging afternoon, Seth decided he'd had enough. He was quitting—no more piano, period! Tom sensed that Seth's attitude had more to do with his immediate frustration and his inability to tolerate being a beginner than with how much his son liked playing the piano. Tom decided that this was a good chance for Seth to learn how to learn. He would assist Seth in developing the confidence that comes with perseverance.

"Seth, I don't think you should quit now," Tom said. "It's important for you to keep taking your lessons. Let's talk about your feelings before you make a decision."

"You never let me decide anything for myself," Seth replied despondently. "It's not fair. I want to quit!" He sounded hurt and angry.

Tom realized that in order to avoid a power struggle, he would have to respond to Seth by including the three guidelines. First, he supported their bond. He neither threatened to withdraw his love (which Seth would have experienced as an emotional abandonment), nor did he attempt to force Seth to practice piano (which would have been an invasion). He simply let Seth express his feelings.

Next, Tom realized that in order for some negotiation to take place, he would have to begin by mirroring and reflecting Seth's feelings. When Seth felt heard, he would be more apt to listen to his dad's point of view and more ready to work out an arrangement that satisfied both father and son.

Mirroring creates an avenue for redress. When their feelings are mirrored, your children sense that you are willing to repair an injury. This is crucial because until they believe their emotions will receive a fair hearing, they will not move on to negotiate the actual content of the problem. Also, when you reflect your children's feelings in a disagreement, they know that their perspective has been considered as well. They don't feel as alone or abandoned.

Using mirroring, Tom said, "I can really see how upset you are, and that you feel it's unfair for me to make you play the piano when you're telling me you don't want to. It seems that trying to learn that new piece has left you really frustrated."

Tom noticed that Seth let out an audible sigh of relief, indicating that he felt understood. Finally Tom was ready to begin the negotiations. He kept in mind guideline 3: Seth was a separate person with a right to his own feelings. To reach a satisfying conclusion for them both, he had to remember that Seth needed to feel that the resolution was fair and equitable. Tom did want his son to be able to play the piano, but he knew it was more important that Seth feel successful at it and enjoy it.

"Look," Tom said, "I don't think it's a good idea to quit because you feel frustrated over a difficult passage. Just the other day, you told me you were really enjoying your lessons, but that you didn't especially enjoy the practicing. I don't want you to quit *now*. I'm going to stay with you and help you learn the difficult part."

"But what if I decide my quitting has nothing to do with the hard part?" Seth replied. "What if I really just don't want to play the piano?"

"Well, I think if you want to quit, you're right, ultimately it should be up to you. However, I want you to continue your lessons for another three months. I'll keep helping you with the hard parts. Then, if you still want to quit, that will be OK with me."

Seth agreed. "I guess that's fair," he told his dad.

Seth did continue his lessons, and with Tom's support he slowly began to gain a better understanding of the learning process. Eventually, Seth stopped playing piano. He switched to the saxophone, which he truly enjoys. In fact, today he is a member of his high-school jazz band.

If Tom had been authoritarian and had ignored Seth's right to have his own feelings, our son would have felt unsupported, and he might have felt forced to either comply or rebel. Had he complied, his anger and resentment most certainly would have interfered with the potential joy of making music. Had he rebelled in order to assume some small measure of control over his own fate, he would have deprived himself of the musical experience altogether. Finally, in rebelling, Seth might also have learned a destructive pattern of behavior. His defiant attempt at separation would have left him disconnected from the sense of self that comes from fully experiencing his own feelings, even in a disagreement. He would have been anchored only to his rebellion.

Tom's support for Seth's separateness also differs from a permissive style of parenting. A permissive parent might say, "OK, you want to quit the piano, fine. It's your choice. I want you to do what you want, whenever you want." This approach leaves kids feeling abandoned, thus weakening the parent-child bond. The child is on his own, with no emotional anchor.

We can see how the three guidelines helped Tom to acknowledge his own legacies and consequently respond more appropriately to Seth's emotional needs. The journal permitted Tom to define his own issues and then use the guidelines to change a painful legacy. Seth experienced himself and his relationship with his father in a different way than Tom had with his dad. Seth was freed from Tom's emotional legacy.

Limit Setting

Your understanding of the Parenting Process facilitates the creation and enforcement of family rules.

Behavior is often the only way children know how to express their feelings. They may be unfamiliar with words that describe emotions, or they may be unconscious of their feelings. As parents it is our job to accept and reflect the emotions we hear or observe in our children, and to set limits if we find their behavior unacceptable.

Setting limits is different from strict discipline, which connotes punishment and control. Setting limits teaches acceptable behavior and protects children, while mirroring lets them maintain their self-esteem. Authoritarian discipline, on the other hand, merely imposes punishment and consequences for behavior that parents don't like, often injuring children's self-worth.

Yet, even though we set limits, children are bound to test them. When you take a stand, your kids may not automatically conform. They will push at your rules and continue unacceptable behavior. This is normal. Testing is a child's way to prove to himself that his parents will remain consistent with their limits. Children experience such consistency as care and protection. With consistent and appropriate limits, children learn that their parents are emotionally available to them. Eventually, they internalize the limits so they can take care of themselves as they grow to maturity.

By using the three guidelines, you can turn limit-setting into an encounter in which you are the custodian of your children's interests and not a combatant in a war of wills. Cynthia, her new husband Robert, and Cynthia's 10-year-old daughter, Gayle, used the Parenting Process to establish and maintain limits and to promote family closeness.

When we met Cynthia, she was distressed about Gayle's behavior. Gayle had discovered a powerful weapon, the ability to disrupt the connection between her mom and her stepfather. When Gayle was angry, she would say, "I'm going to throw a book at you, and you can't do anything to stop me!" Robert would leave the room without a comment.

Robert wanted very much for Gayle to like him and accept him into the newly structured family. Robert avoided setting limits with Gayle; he thought this would minimize his mistakes and increase his chances of being accepted. His solution was to let his wife do all the parenting.

Cynthia felt overburdened and angry with Robert for abdicating responsibility and refusing to set limits with Gayle. Since childhood, Cynthia had taken the role of mother's helper. She was the good girl, responsible for the well-being of other family members. Now here she was, a grown woman, reliving this role with Robert and Gayle.

During their first consultation, Robert described what had transpired when he tried to enforce Cynthia's rules. Robert asked Gayle to finish her homework before watching TV:

Gayle: I don't want to do my homework now. I'll do it later.

Robert: Wouldn't it be better if you did it before TV?

Gayle: No. I want to watch The Cosby Show.

Robert: I want you to listen to me.

Gayle: You're not my dad. You can't tell me what to do, and I don't have to listen to you if I don't want to.

At this point Robert left the room, feeling helpless.

Tom asked Robert how old he felt during this incident. Robert laughed and said he felt like a frustrated three-year-old. Tom asked if Robert could remember what he was aware of in his body during this incident. Robert told us he felt his heart pounding and that his jaw had been very tight. He also remembered holding his breath. He hadn't felt quite all there. He felt detached. These are the classic signs of fragmentation (see chapter 3).

Indeed, Gayle's stubborn behavior had taken Robert back to his childhood. How could Robert cope the next time this occurred? We advised him to take time out, the next time he felt fragmented. During this break, he could take several deep, relaxing breaths. Then, we recommended he look around the room and name several objects and their color in rapid succession. This helps to bring one back from a fragmented state into the here and now. Finally, we suggested that when he got home he write in his journal, matching the emotions from the argument with those evoked from his childhood.

The following week Robert brought in his journal, in which he had written:

"I remember feeling helpless and criticized with my mom a lot, and the sensations in my body are similar, too. I can't recall any specific example, but the feeling sure is the same: It was hard to get her to pay attention to me, and when she did, she was often angry with me or critical."

Once Robert had connected his feelings toward Gayle with his childhood experiences with his mother, he was ready to absorb the themes of the Parenting Process. These he learned well.

Not surprisingly, the following week the conflict between Gayle and Robert resurfaced when The Cosby Show came on. This time, Robert handled the situation more successfully:

Robert: Gayle, I remember you made an agreement with your mom and me: No TV before your homework is finished.

Gayle: I don't care if we made an agreement. You are not my dad. You can't tell me what to do.

Robert felt his jaw begin to tighten. But instead of helplessly walking out of the room (which would have threatened the bond between them), he took a deep breath. Then, he remembered to mirror Gayle.

Robert: You know, I can really see how mad you are, and that you are upset about having to miss your favorite television show.

Gayle: I am mad. I'd rather watch TV than do this stupid book report.

Robert continued to mirror Gayle's feelings of resentment.

Robert: Sometimes it is hard to do homework when
            you want to have fun instead. Come on, I
            want you to get started now.

Gayle: (In a sulky and resentful voice) Oh, all right.
            But I don't really want to.

Robert, keeping guideline 3 in mind, allowed Gayle to have her own separate feelings of resentment. He didn't try to force Gayle to be in a better mood or to be happy about having to do her homework.

It's important for you to remember that setting limits involves changing your child's *behavior,* not her feelings. When you continue to mirror, rather than engaging in a struggle to force your children to change their feelings, your interactions will be more satisfying for all concerned. Youngsters' feelings change as a natural consequence of your relating to them respectfully.

Appropriate Consequences

Limit-setting is more likely to be effective when you use the guidelines of the Parenting Process to create and enforce appropriate consequences. Guideline 1 insures that the consequences will not threaten to emotionally invade or abandon your child, therefore protecting the bond. Guideline 2 allows you to understand and validate your children's emotional experience during the limit-setting process. Guideline 3 gives you the opportunity to set limits and consequences without damaging your youngsters' self-esteem. When you recognize your separate boundaries, you won't take personally your children's misbehavior. Your youngster's actions are information about their experience, not about who you are. Thus, the consequences that you create will not come from your guilt or inappropriate anger and fragmentation but from your sense of what is appropriate in the here and now.

Appropriate consequences support limit-setting by demonstrating to your child that undesirable behavior will bring an undesirable result. An appropriate consequence:

- is connected to the child's behavior
- matters to the child
- is of short duration

Bev may tell eight-year-old Ricky for example, "I understand you're unhappy about having to go to bed, but if you continue to fight about your bedtime tonight, you will lose your TV privileges tomorrow evening." Bev has set a limit and created an appropriate consequence. First of all, TV watching was related to Ricky's behavior. Second, TV was important to the boy. Finally, he would lose his privilege for only one night, not the rest of his life. If Ricky continues to fight Bev, she must be prepared to follow through. If Bev fails to do so, Ricky's behavior would continue and would even escalate. When you choose a consequence to support a rule, it is important to follow through consistently. Otherwise children will not believe you and may increase their testing.

Behavioral psychologists, in studying how people learn behavior, explain why this is so. Parents reinforce their children's behavior in three ways:

- *Positive reinforcement:* giving positive rewards and attention to reinforce behavior.

- *Negative reinforcement:* giving negative consequences to extinguish or stop behavior,

- *Intermittent reinforcement:* behavior is reinforced either positively or negatively, but inconsistently. Intermittent reinforcement develops the strongest behavior patterns of all because kids never know how you will respond. They keep testing to try and receive a consistent response.

Testing is often your child's attempt to see if you will hold the line. Since intermittent reinforcement is the strongest kind of reinforcement, it is important that you be as consistent as possible with both your limits and your consequences in order to avoid unnecessary testing.

Marilyn, mother of four-year-old Brian, came to one of our workshops with this problem. She and Brian rented rooms in a house with two other adults. Marilyn was worried that if Brian made too much commotion about bedtime, her roommates would be upset and would ask them to leave. This caused Marilyn to vacillate between being very severe with Brian and caving in to his demands to stay up later in order to quiet him. This vacillation increased Brian's testing, and the volume of their bedtime fights escalated.

We told Marilyn about the importance of consistency. We encouraged her to enlist her roommates' cooperation and to inform them that for the next few nights the fighting might get worse because she was going to hold the line about bedtime. In fact, the first couple of nights that Marilyn remained firm, Brian put up quite a fuss. By the third night, however, he began to lessen his opposition, and by the end of the week he was cooperatively going to bed.

Resolving Sibling Conflicts

Patricia and Tony came to our workshop because their two children, Dean (age 12) and Beth (age 8) were constantly fighting over whether Dean would let Beth play with him. Sometimes he would, but at other times he was mean to his sister, calling her names and teasing her. She would beg him, "Please, please, pretty please, let me play with you." He would either give in, and be resentful or push her away with more name-calling and teasing. Patricia and Tony felt they had told both kids to be nice to each other at least a million times and were ready to tear their hair out!

We taught Patricia and Tony the Parenting Process. They came back the following week, excited by the results. Tony explained how they had used the guidelines to resolve the fighting and set limits and consequences.

Tony and Patricia were in the den when they heard wild screaming coming from the bedroom. They went together to see what was going on.

Beth: (Wailing) You hurt my feelings! I am not a creep! I am not a baby!

Dean: (In a voice louder than Beth's) You are too a baby! Look at how you are crying! I don't play with stupid babies!

Tony: I am going to stop the two of you from fighting. Beth, come and sit with me. Dean, tell us what's going on.

After listening to Dean's story, Patricia said, "Dean, you may not call your sister names and tease her. If you don't want to play with Beth, you don't have to. You can say yes or no to her. I hear that you are not always in the mood. However, if you keep teasing her instead of just telling her no, I won't let you play with your computer game tonight."

Tony added, "Beth, you have a part in this, too. It hurts your feelings when Dean says he doesn't want to play with you. But when he says no, you ask him again and again. Mom made a rule: Dean can say yes or no, but he can't call you names and tease you. You have to learn to respect his decision. I understand that it is difficult for you when he says no, but it's not OK to bug him. Come to me or Mom, and we'll help you find something else to do. I know that if you respect Dean's right to say no, sometimes he will even say yes."

This was Tony and Patricia's first step out of the confusion. Everyone's boundaries were respected. Neither parent felt so overwhelmed that he or she flew into a rage (which had happened many times before), nor did they abandon or invade either child. Tony and Patricia listened and reflected both kids' feelings, without making either of them feel bad or wrong. They allowed each to have his or her own feelings and needs. Patricia and Tony used "I" statements and set good limits on behavior. They created consequences that were effective without being too severe. This is the Parenting Process in action.

Interrupting the Legacy

Jennifer and Jeff were referred to us by their family physician, who felt they would benefit from a parenting seminar after they had expressed their concerns about their four-year-old, Naomi. She had recently revived the habit of carrying her security blanket and sucking her thumb.

In many ways, Jennifer and Jeff were typical of today's busy professional parents. Jennifer was a successful accountant in her early 40s, a workaholic who was a junior partner at a prestigious accounting firm. She had only missed one month of work after her daughter was born. Her husband, Jeff, was a prominent orthopedist at the county hospital.

You might say that Naomi was a thoroughly planned baby. Her mom and dad not only scheduled her conception but, long before her birth, created a blueprint detailing every facet of the enriched life she would lead. They knew which tot gym she would attend, researched swimming lessons for infants, and placed her on the waiting list of the highest-rated preschool in town two months before her birth.

Naomi might not have known it, but her parents were sure that she was destined to be the brightest, most successful member of the class of 2008. About the only thing they hadn't settled was which university she would attend, her mother's or her father's.

In attempting to create a perfect child and in predetermining all the experiences they would provide her, Jennifer and Jeff forgot to leave room for what Naomi wanted. Naomi had regressed to an earlier stage to protect herself from her parents' overwhelming demands to perform. By retreating into her three-year-old self, she sought escape from the pressures of her four-year-old life. Naomi was a preschool stress victim.

Jennifer and Jeff had similar backgrounds. They had been raised in families that expected and demanded high performance. Jeff hadn't even decided to go to medical school; it was always assumed he would follow in his father's footsteps. Jennifer's mom and dad had always pushed her to be the best and not to settle for "anything less than perfection."

The high standards that were set for Jeff and Jennifer were not bad in themselves, but neither of their parents had been attuned to them. They only felt love and recognition when they performed well.

Once we had inquired about Jennifer and Jeff's family histories and about Naomi's current life, it was clear that these parents were handing down their legacy of high performance to their daughter. We told them that Naomi's behavior served as a message to them: "I am under too much pressure." In fact, it sounded to us as if everyone in the family was under too much pressure.

After Jeff and Jennifer learned the Parenting Process, they began to appreciate Naomi's regressive behavior not as a problem but rather as her attempt to communicate her feelings. When they learned about bonding through guideline 1, they realized that a bond that doesn't allow for play, spontaneity, and a child's innate creativity and fantasy life is more of a chain. By following guideline 1, Jennifer and Jeff were able to change their controlling attitude toward their daughter.

A sure way to invade children is to attempt to control their lives. It is one thing to provide your child with stimulating, enjoyable, even appropriately demanding experiences, and another to overburden her by over-scheduling all of her free time. Play is the single most important experience for kids. Children learn about who they are, about peer relationships, and about the world through play.

Moreover, because of their family legacies, Jeff and Jennifer had never been mirrored, nor had they ever learned to mirror their child. Instead, they concentrated on performance. Accepting guideline 2 gave them a way to actively listen that would help them get to know the real Naomi. As these parents attended to their child's emotional needs, they discovered that she was not much interested in dance class or computer training. She wanted to play dress-up with her school friends. She wanted to fill a page or two with colors and shapes that weren't judged on how well they resembled objects. She wanted to play in her sand box, running the hose and making mud pies.

As her parents began to understand Naomi's real likes and dislikes, she began to feel seen and heard. She grew emotionally more secure. Soon the thumb came out of her mouth, and the blanket returned to the drawer.

Until this crisis, Jeff and Jennifer had been teaching Naomi their way of living. Their lives were filled with structured activities and the push for accomplishment. We imagined these two busy parents had been heading for their own health crisis. But unlike Naomi, who could turn into a baby to protect herself from feeling over-whelmed, adult bodies and adult psyches wishing to pro-test such conditions often choose serious illness as their escape.

Naomi and her parents needed time to be together. They shifted away from letting accomplishments take priority over their emotional and family life, toward having fun as a family. Guideline 3 helped them respect emotional differences and allow Naomi her four-year-old needs and feelings. No longer a burned-out, overcompliant child, Naomi was now able to let her own affinities and preferences surface.

We should note, however, that this process occurred in fits and starts. It took several months for Jeff and Jennifer to integrate the Parenting Process into their lives. Occasionally, they would veer off the track and begin to place too much pressure on Naomi. Predictably, she would regress. She didn't return to thumb-sucking, but she would become withdrawn and "little" under these circumstances. Mom and Dad learned to recognize this behavior not as a crisis or as bad behavior but as a signal, an indication of the state of Naomi's emotional well-being. This family learned to make time for each other, have fun, and enjoy themselves.

The three Parenting Process guidelines work together harmoniously. They are the building blocks for establishing a sense of well-being in your children and ultimately in your entire family.

The Parenting Process can be the basis for providing support for intimacy and autonomy in your family. Taken together, the guidelines offer you a tool to help you analyze the emotional transactions in your family, diagnose problems, discover the missing pieces, and provide a way to repair injuries and hurt feelings. Thus, painful family legacies need not be handed down. The Parenting Process is a prescription for healthy family functioning. As you incorporate the Parenting Process into your family life, you will not only interrupt the transfer of your childhood injuries but also teach your children how to parent.

9

Looking Toward the Future

Peace between countries must rest on the solid foundation of love between individuals.

Mahatma Gandhi

*T*he Parenting Process is a way for parents to change their families by introducing flexibility and equality into family life. There is a natural progression from childhood experience within our families to independent lives as adults in society. As adults, our children will encounter many problems, including rigid institutions, injustice, poverty, political instability, and a changing global economy. Instead of pushing your child to merely adapt and adjust to parental authority, the Parenting Process gives your children a real voice in family life. Youngsters who have experienced the Parenting Process will be better prepared to change the society in which they must live as adults.

Equality

When children have the everyday experience of being treated fairly, equality becomes a reality, rather than an intellectual ideal. We tend to treat others the way we have been treated. All family members, regardless of their size, age, or gender, should be treated as emotional equals. The Parenting Process insures that the emotional experience of every family member will be respected and valued, even when there are differences.

We believe that children who grow up in families that have utilized the Parenting Process will participate in society with the ability to treat others fairly in spite of such differences as race, sex, religion, or economic status because these children have had the direct experience of mutual respect.

Families and Flexibility

The Parenting Process is an outline for flexible family relations. As you incorporate the guidelines, you all learn to relate to each other without relinquishing your needs. So, instead of handing down a rigid set of relationship patterns and roles, you can create new patterns of relating. These are based on your family's present needs and not on ancient history. Through such conscious parenting, you can enjoy warmth, intimacy, joy, and a respect for each family member's uniqueness—the hallmarks of a satisfying home life.

The Parenting Process and Social Change

Social change can begin within the family. It is within the home that parents create emotionally healthy individuals. By using the Parenting Process, you'll be able to raise kids who enjoy high self-esteem. When children possess authentic self-worth, they will want to recreate this positive sensation in their adult lives and relationships.

As a result of the Parenting Process, we envision children who are neither innocent and naive nor pessimistic and cynical. Rather, we foresee individuals who are problem solvers. They will carry their good feelings into the world, changing it to reflect their personal hopes and desires, as well as their trust in humankind.

Families and Community

We all need the ability to respond to the shifts in feelings that occur in our family life as well as the changing priorities of our communities and society. When institutions such as local, state, and federal bureaucracies become rigid and unresponsive, we must look to individuals or groups of individuals to serve as agents of change. The Parenting Process prepares children to influence the responsiveness of just such heartless institutions, because these youngsters have learned flexibility and equality in their own families.

The health of the larger community depends on the emotional health of our families, which, in turn, owe their well-being to the adults and children that make up these families.

The vehicle through which we experience life is our individual perspective—our self. We cannot, however, entirely separate our well-being from that of others. This lesson is one we must learn whether we are talking about our family, our community, our country, or our world. We often forget that we exist in a web of bondedness with all who share our planet. When we look at photographs of the earth seen from space, it is easy to see how national boundaries are often arbitrary and artificial. Whether they are individual or national, boundaries need to be flexible to allow for both autonomy and connection. The problem for the community of nations is the same as that for individuals within a family: how to maintain independence and uniqueness while nourishing unity and connectedness among all people.

For hope, we must return to the individual experience of separateness and empathic connection. This individual experience takes place in the family. We respond to the call of Nikos Kazantzakis in *Saviors of God* when he said, "And I strive to discover how to signal my companions . . . to say in time a simple word, a password, like conspirators: Let us unite, let us hold each other tightly, let us merge our hearts, let us create for earth a brain and a heart, let us give a human meaning to the superhuman struggle."

Bibliography

Brazelton, T.B., M.D. and Cramer, B.G., M.D. (1990) The Earliest Relationship. New York: Addison Wesley.

Bowlby (1969) Attachment. Vol. 1. New York: Basic Books.

Chodorow, N. (1978) The Reproduction of Mothering, Psychoanalysis and the Sociology of Gender. Berkeley and Los Angeles: University of California Press.

Dinnerstein, D. (1976) The Mermaid and the Minotaur. New York: Harper & Row

Forward, S. (1989) Toxic Parents. New York: Bantam Books.

Gilligan, C. (1982) In a Different Voice. Cambridge: Harvard University Press.

Kaplan, L. J. (1978) Oneness & Separateness: From Infant to Individual. New York: Simon & Schuster.

Kazantzakis, N. (1960) Saviors of God. Translated by Kimon Friar. New York: Simon and Schuster.

Kohut, H. (1984) How Does Analysis Cure? London: University of Chicago Press.

Mahler, M. S., Pine, F. and Bergman, A. (1975) The Psychological Birth of the Human Infant. New York: Basic Books.

May, Rollo. (1975) The Courage to Create. New York: Bantam Books

Miller, A. (1981) The Drama of the Gifted Child. New York: Basic Books.

Neill, A. S. (1960) Summerhill—A Radical Approach to Childrearing. New York: Hart Publishing Co.

Neill, A. S. (1966) Freedom—Not License! New York: Hart Publishing Company, Inc.

Public Broadcasting System, KCET, *Nova,* Life's First Feelings. Produced by James Lipscomb and Bill Wander, hosted by Dr. Tom Cottle.

Rogers, C. R. (1961) On Becoming a Person. Boston: Houghton Mifflin Company.

Rosenberg, J. L., with Rand, M. L. (1985) Body, Self & Soul. Atlanta: Humanics Limited.

Stern, D.N. (1985) The Interpersonal World of the Infant. New York: Basic Books.

Wells, H.G. (1928) The Open Conspiracy: Blueprints for a World Revolution.

Index